JAPANESE ZEN GARDENS

YOKO KAWAGUCHI

JAPANESE ZEN GARDENS

PHOTOGRAPHS BY
ALEX RAMSAY

F
FRANCES LINCOLN LIMITED
PUBLISHERS

Frances Lincoln Limited
www.franceslincoln.com

Japanese Zen Gardens
Copyright © Frances Lincoln Limited 2014
Text copyright © Yoko Kamaguchi 2014
Photographs copyright © Alex Ramsay 2014,
except those listed on page 208
Garden plans copyright © Kathryn Pinker 2014

British Library Cataloguing in Publication Data
A catalogue record for this book is available
from the British Library

ISBN 978-0-7112-3447-5

Printed in China

9 8 7 6 5 4 3 2 1

In accordance with conventional Japanese
usage, in this book personal names are given
surname first. In subsequent references,
historical figures are called by their forenames,
contemporary people by their surnames.

RIGHT The effect of an ink-brush painting
is produced when autumn mists hang
over the distant hills behind Tenryū-ji's
pond garden, which features a spectacular,
dry-waterfall arrangement.

HALF-TITLE PAGE A glimpse of Japanese
maples in autumn colour is framed by
the pillars of Nanzen-ji's *sanmon* (main
inner gateway).

OPPOSITE TITLE PAGE Old paving stones
have been reused by the twentieth-
century garden architect Shigemori
Mirei to create a chequerboard pattern
in the north garden of Tōfuku-ji's *hōjō*
(abbot's hall).

CONTENTS

FOREWORD

Zen Buddhist temples have played an important role in the development of garden styles in Japan. They provided a cultural milieu in which Japanese garden traditions came in contact with new influences from China. Japanese Zen monks cultivated a great interest in Chinese art, particularly calligraphy and ink-brush painting, and the aesthetics of Chinese landscape painting – its use of space and perspective – had a profound effect on the design of Japanese landscape gardens.

It is from this cultural melting pot that the Japanese *kare-sansui* (dry-landscape) garden developed – the great example of which is the famous stone garden at Ryōan-ji. The major stylistic innovation of using raked gravel to represent a body of water made it possible to create the illusion of space and distance in the smallest of gardens, such as those that were constructed around the *hōjō* (abbot's hall), the spiritual hub of the Zen Buddhist temple. By the eighteenth century, the flat gravelled garden was a recognised garden style in Japan and was being adopted outside the specific context of Buddhist temples. A revival of interest in this type of garden during the twentieth century has influenced modern Japanese garden design: for example, the development of very small, enclosed courtyard gardens, known as *tsubo-niwa*.

The *kare-sansui* garden is known outside Japan as the 'Zen garden', but in Japan the style is no longer narrowly defined by its Zen associations. Meanwhile, at Zen Buddhist temples, other styles of garden have emerged. For example, the ceremony of tea drinking, originally introduced from China, developed a distinctly Japanese ethos under the influence of Zen Buddhism, and Zen temple gardens, in turn, absorbed elements of the tea garden. Zen temple gardens have always been open to, and have assimilated, cultural influences in a very creative way.

Yoko Kawaguchi

INTRODUCTION

One of the most enigmatic gardens in the world must be the stone-and-gravel, dry garden that faces the south front of the *hōjō* (abbot's hall) at Ryōan-ji, a Zen Buddhist temple located among the foothills to the north of the ancient Japanese capital Kyōto. It is a walled garden laid with evenly raked, fine white gravel, on which five groups of rocks, totalling fifteen in number, have been arranged, each on its own small, carefully defined island of moss. It seems the very antithesis of what a garden ought to be. Indeed, it appears to lack the one thing that most people would most associate with gardens – plants – unless one includes the moss, which in many cultures is considered a weed.

Visitors to Ryōan-ji have, for centuries, sought to find a meaning in the fifteen stones. The fact that the garden is located within the precincts of a Zen Buddhist temple has, without doubt, contributed to its mystique. This has encouraged speculation that the abstract design of the garden might in some way reflect a religious revelation – perhaps even the very essence of *satori*,

that spiritual enlightenment that all Buddhists seek. So close an association has been formed between this abstract style and the supposedly esoteric truths embedded in Buddhism that the term 'Zen garden', outside Japan, has become all but synonymous with this type of stone-and-gravel, dry garden.

In fact, however, the style constitutes a stage in the evolution of the Japanese Zen temple garden. The tradition of having gardens within the grounds of Zen Buddhist temples has a long and rich history in Japan. It owes a great deal to various Chinese cultural influences – Buddhist and otherwise. It also draws heavily on long-standing, native Japanese customs and preferences. It was affected by the fortunes of the temples themselves, which were often intimately connected with the rise and fall of the political prestige of their powerful patrons.

The Ryōan-ji garden is not a 'typical' Zen garden, because many different styles of gardens are found at Japanese Zen temples. Nor is the *kare-sansui*

600 AD	900	1100	1200	1250	1300

JAPAN
794: A new imperial capital is established at Heian-kyō (modern-day Kyōto)

CHINA
618: Fall of the Sui dynasty; birth of the Tang dynasty

EUROPE
800: Charlemagne is crowned 'Emperor of the Romans' by Pope Leo III

JAPAN
1050–c.1090: The oldest surviving gardening manual in Japan, the *Sakutei-ki*, is compiled

CHINA
907: Fall of the Tang dynasty
960: Birth of the Song dynasty

EUROPE
962: Otto I is crowned Holy Roman Emperor
1066: Norman Conquest of England (BELOW)

JAPAN
1185: The Minamoto clan seizes power in Japan
1191: Myōan Yōsai returns from China and spreads Rinzai Zen Buddhism

CHINA
1127: Song dynasty loses control of northern China, and re-establishes itself south of the Yangtze river (Southern Song dynasty) (BELOW)

JAPAN
1202: Myōan Yōsai founds Kennin-ji in Kyōto
1243: Enni Bennen becomes the first abbot of Tōfuku-ji in Kyōto
1246: The Chinese Chán monk Lan-ch'i Tao-lung (Rankei Dōryū) arrives in Japan

CHINA
1206: The Mongol Empire established under Genghis Khan

EUROPE
1215: Magna Carta is sealed by King John, of England, at Runnymede

JAPAN
1274: The emperor Kameyama abdicates
1291: Mukan Fumon, third abbot of Tōfuku-ji, builds Ryōgin-an; he is also appointed abbot of the new temple (later renamed Nanzen-ji), which the former emperor Kameyama founds on the site of his villa Zenrinji-dono; Mukan Fumon dies at Ryōgin-an at the end of the year

CHINA
1271: Kublai Khan establishes the Yuan dynasty and becomes emperor of China
1271–1295: Marco Polo travels to China
1279: Fall of Southern Song dynasty and the unification of China under Kublai Khan

EUROPE
1299: Birth of the Ottoman Empire

JAPAN
1315: The Rinzai Zen monk Shūhō Myōchō founds a temple in north Kyōto, which later becomes Daitoku-ji
1333: Fall of the Kamakura shogunate; the emperor Go-Daigo assumes power
1336: Go-Daigo flees Kyōto and Ashikaga Taka'uji assumes power (beginnings of the Ashikaga shogunate, otherwise known as the Muromachi shogunate)
1337: An imperial villa in Kyōto belonging to the former emperor Hanazono is designated to become the Rinzai Zen temple, Myōshin-ji
1338: Ashikaga Taka'uji becomes shogun
1339: Musō Soseki refounds Saihō-ji as a Rinzai Zen temple; death of Go-Daigo; Ashikaga Taka'uji and his brother Tadayoshi found Tenryū-ji

EUROPE
c.1304–1321: Dante writes *The Divine Comedy*
1333–1391: Creation of the gardens at Alhambra Palace, Granada (LEFT)
1337–1453: Hundred Years War between England and France

RIGHT A waterfall, the raised head of a dragon and Shumisen (the mountain at the centre of the Buddhist universe) are some of the interpretations that have been inspired by the leaning stone in the north garden of the *hōjō* (abbot's hall) at Ryōgen-in.

PRECEDING PAGES The white gravel in the west *hōjō* garden at Taizō-in symbolises a lake flowing past an island and on into the distant horizon. Beyond the island, on the left, there is an upright stone representing the outstretched wing of a crane. A remote mountain range is indicated by the boulders arrayed along the far left edge of the garden.

1350	1400	1450	1500	1550

JAPAN
1368: Ashikaga Yoshimitsu becomes shogun
1394: Yoshimitsu abdicates
1397: Yoshimitsu begins building his new villa, Kitayama-dono

CHINA
1368: Fall of the Yuan dynasty; birth of the Ming dynasty (BELOW)

EUROPE
1378-1417: The Great Schism splits the Roman Catholic Church

JAPAN
1408: Death of Ashikaga Yoshimitsu
1420: Yoshimitsu's Kitayama-dono becomes the Rokuon-ji (Temple of the Golden Pavilion) (BELOW)
1449: Ashikaga Yoshimasa becomes shōgun

JAPAN
1467–1477: Ōnin War
1467–1469: The artist–monk Sesshū visits China
1473: Ashikaga Yoshimasa abdicates
1474: Ikkyū Sōjun is appointed abbot of Daitoku-ji and begins its reconstruction
1482: Ashikaga Yoshimasa begins building his new villa, Higashiyama-dono
1490: Yoshimasa dies, and his villa becomes Jishō-in, soon renamed Jishō-ji

EUROPE
c.1450: Johannes Gutenberg sets up his printing press at Mainz
1453: Fall of Constantinople to the Ottoman Turks
1492: Christopher Columbus reaches the Americas

JAPAN
1509: Kogaku Sōkō becomes abbot of Daitoku-ji and founds the sub-temple Daisen-in
1543: Two shipwrecked Portuguese traders become the first Europeans to reach Japan
1549: The Catholic missionary Francis Xavier arrives in Japan

EUROPE
1517: Martin Luther presents his Ninety-Five Theses, triggering the start of the Protestant Reformation (BELOW)

JAPAN
1573: Oda Nobunaga forces the last Ashikaga shogun from Kyōto
1582: Death of Oda Nobunaga
1586–1587: Toyotomi Hideyoshi builds his Jurakudai Palace at Kyōto
1590: Hideyoshi unifies Japan
1591: The celebrated tea master Sen no Rikyū is ordered by Hideyoshi to take his own life
1595: The Jurakudai Palace is demolished
1596: Reconstruction of Hideyoshi's Fushimi Castle begins after its destruction in an earthquake
1598: Death of Hideyoshi at Fushimi Castle

EUROPE
1558: Elizabeth I becomes Queen of England (BELOW)
1559: Architect Pirro Ligorio begins work on the Villa d'Este gardens, Tivoli

A weeping cherry drapes its branches over the south wall of the stone garden at Ryōan-ji. This wall is of a type known in Japan as *abura-dobei*, in which clay has been mixed with rapeseed oil and brine for extra durability.

1600	1625	1650	1700	1750

JAPAN
1600: Tokugawa Ieyasu seizes power (beginnings of the Tokugawa shogunate based at Edo, later Tōkyō)
1603: Ieyasu is appointed shogun
1605: Ieyasu cedes his position to his son Hidetada but retains political control; Ishin Sūden becomes abbot of Nanzen-ji
1606: Toyotomi Hideyoshi's widow founds Kōdai-ji
1613: Christianity is proscribed throughout Japan
1615: The *daimyō* and eminent tea master Furuta Oribe is ordered by the shogunate to take his own life
c.**1615**–*c*.**1640**: Restoration of Jishō-ji (Temple of the Silver Pavilion)
1616: Death of Tokugawa Ieyasu

EUROPE
1620: The *Mayflower* takes the Pilgrim Fathers to New England

JAPAN
1626: Ishin Sūden begins renovating Konchi-in
c.**1630**: The south garden of the *dai-hōjō* at Nanzen-ji begun
1632: The south *hōjō* garden at Konchi-in is completed
1636: A new *hōjō* is built at Daitoku-ji
1639: Portuguese shipping is banned; the Dutch and the Chinese become Japan's only two remaining foreign trading partners

EUROPE
1649: Execution of Charles I of England (BELOW)

JAPAN
1663: Construction of Jikō-in begins
1678: Entsū-ji is founded on the site of the former emperor Go-Mizuno'o's Hata'eda villa.
1690: German physician and naturalist Engelbert Kaempfer arrives in Japan as an employee of the Dutch East India Company (–1692).

EUROPE
1656–1661: André Le Nôtre designs the gardens at Vaux-le-Vicomte for Nicolas Fouquet, Louis XIV's finance minister (BELOW)
1660: Restoration of the monarchy in England

EUROPE
1715–49: The English landscape gardens at Stowe, in Buckinghamshire, are created (BELOW)

JAPAN
1775: Swedish botanist Carl Peter Thunberg arrives in Japan as an employee of the Dutch East India Company (–1777)
1780, 1787, 1799: Ritōken Akisato publishes illustrated guide books to Kyōto

EUROPE
1761: William Chambers builds the Chinese pagoda at Kew (BELOW)
1764: Lancelot 'Capability' Brown redesigns the park at Blenheim Palace, Oxfordshire
1789: The French Revolution begins

(dry-landscape) style, of which the Ryōan-ji garden is an example, exclusively associated in Japanese culture with Zen Buddhism. Indeed, nor are there distinctive styles of garden so specific to Zen Buddhist temples that they can still be called 'Zen gardens' when they are not actually located at one of these temples. If a garden could be described at all as a 'Zen garden', it is not so much on stylistic grounds but in the spirit in which the visitor approaches it.

Zen Buddhist temples in Japan developed a tradition of having a garden facing the three main rooms of the *hōjō* (abbot's hall). These were the rooms in which the abbot offered his prayers, conducted religious ceremonies, instructed his acolytes and met the temple's patrons and lay worshippers. Although it is a moot point whether the garden was actually used as a practical aid to meditation, it certainly had an important role in creating the spiritual ambience of the *hōjō*, and the visitor for his part would have approached the garden in a frame of mind determined by his awareness of where he was. Visiting a temple can lift a person out of the rut of everyday existence.

A domestic garden can equally be a 'Zen garden' in so much as it has a spiritual or religious significance for its owner, although he or she may be the only one who views it in that light. The spiritual effect of a garden can be a separate issue from that of interpretation, and is often of a very personal nature.

An understanding of how gardens developed in the context of Japanese Zen Buddhist temples is an important step in exploring the idea of Zen gardens in general. *Japanese Zen Gardens* sets out to trace this history and to show how the blending of diverse cultural influences — ancient and modern, native and foreign — has produced a rich tradition of garden design that has gone on to have influence far beyond the walls of Buddhist temples. The book also considers in greater detail some of the chief imagery that recurs in Zen temple gardens, such as the *ryūmon-baku* (dragon-gate waterfall). In addition, there is a section examining the relationship between Zen temple gardens and Japanese tea gardens, as well as information on some plants that are important to these gardens.

1800

JAPAN
1814: The monk Tōboku Sōho creates gardens for Tōkai-an
1823: German physician and botanist Philipp Franz von Siebold arrives in Japan as an employee of the Dutch East India Company
1829: Siebold is expelled from Japan after being suspected of acting as a spy for foreign powers

EUROPE
1804: Napoleon Bonaparte crowned emperor of the French (BELOW)
1815: Battle of Waterloo
1837: Victoria ascends British throne

1850

JAPAN
1853: Commodore Matthew C. Perry's squadron of American warships arrives in Japanese waters
1867: Fall of the Tokugawa shogunate
1868: The emperor Meiji assumes power; a mass anti-Buddhist movement is sparked off by a series of government edicts ordering the separation of Shinto and Buddhist practices
1869: Tōkyō (formerly Edo) becomes the official capital of Japan
1894–95: First Sino-Japanese War

EUROPE
1852: Louis-Napoléon Bonaparte crowned Napoléon III, emperor of the French
1870: Franco-Prussian War (BELOW)
1871: Unification of Germany
***c*.1860–*c*.1914**: Vogue for *Japonisme* in Europe and America
1885: Gilbert and Sullivan's *The Mikado* premieres at the Savoy Theatre, London

1900

JAPAN
1904–1905: Russo-Japanese War
1910: Japan annexes Korea
1931: Japanese invasion of Manchuria
1936–1938: Shigemori Mirei conducts his first series of surveys of historical gardens
1937–1945: Second Sino-Japanese War
1939: Shigemori Mirei creates gardens for Tōfuku-ji and restores the south *hōjō* garden at Funda-in
1941–1945: Pacific War

EUROPE
1914–1918: First World War
1939: Second World War begins in Europe (–1945) (BELOW)

1950–

JAPAN
1961: Nakane Kinsaku restores the north-east and east *hōjō* gardens at Daisen-in at Daitokuji
1964: Shigemori Mirei creates gardens for Ryōgin-an at Tōfuku-ji (BELOW)
1971: Shigemori Mirei conducts his second series of surveys of historic gardens
1975: Elizabeth II visits Ryōan-ji during a state visit to Japan
1994: Saihō-ji, Tenryū-ji, Ryōan-ji, Rokuon-ji and Jishō-ji are included among a group of seventeen sites in and around Kyōto given UNESCO World Heritage status
2006: Kitayama Yasuo creates courtyard gardens for Kennin-ji

PART ONE

JAPANESE ZEN TEMPLES
AND THEIR GARDENS:
AN HISTORICAL OVERVIEW

JAPANESE ZEN TEMPLES AND THEIR GARDENS: AN HISTORICAL OVERVIEW

NANZEN-IN

Without the patronage of Zen Buddhist temples by the aristocracy and the military elite during the thirteenth and fourteenth centuries, Japan might never have produced the extensive temple garden tradition for which it is now so renowned. The first Zen temple to be built in Japan is said to have been Danrin-ji, in Kyōto, founded in the first half of the ninth century by the dowager empress Tachibana no Kachiko, who invited a Chinese monk to come to Japan and teach Chán (the Chinese term for Zen) Buddhism. However, Zen Buddhism did not truly begin to take root in Japan until the second half of the twelfth century, and this was through the influence of the Japanese monk Myōan Yōsai (otherwise known as Eisai), who travelled to China and became a Chán master in 1191.

Aspects of Zen teaching have always been part of the Buddhist tradition, but Chán emerged as a distinct branch of Buddhism during China's Tang dynasty. Supposedly, it was introduced into China from India in the first half of the sixth century by the semi-legendary monk Bodhidharma (known as Daruma in Japan). Chán gained a considerable following among China's political elite, but suffered under Emperor Wu-tsung's persecution of Buddhist institutions in the middle of the ninth century. It did, however, find new life in the provinces. One of the most influential Chán masters to emerge out of this milieu was Línjì Yìxuán (known as Rinzai Giken in Japan), whose teachings became the basis for the Línjì school of Chán Buddhism. This became the dominant branch of Chán once political stability in China was re-established in 960 under the new Song dynasty. It was the Línjì school of Chán Buddhism that Myōan Yōsai brought back to Japan, where it became known as the Rinzai school.

At that time, Japan was going through a politically tumultuous period. The *bushi* (military class) had already wrested power from the imperial court.

LEFT Two wooden pillars of Nanzen-in's *hōjō* (abbot's hall) frame a view of the stone representing a crane's outstretched wing in the temple's south garden.

PREVIOUS PAGE Nanzen-in's south *hōjō* garden is dominated by a symbolic turtle island (right) and a crane island, behind which, to the left, there is an ancient man-made waterfall designed to resemble a mountain cascade.

Rivalry between the two principal *bushi* clans – the Taira and the Minamoto – culminated in 1185 in the latter defeating the former, and setting up its seat of government at Kamakura in east Japan. The imperial court, meanwhile, remained in Kyōto.

After his return from China in 1191, Myōan Yōsai succeeded in winning the following of the second Kamakura shogun, and with his backing Yōsai was able to found the Kennin-ji temple in Kyōto in 1202. Kennin-ji is, today, a Rinzai Zen temple, but at the time of its foundation it taught Rinzai Zen Buddhism alongside two established schools of Buddhism – Tendai and Shingon. The same approach was taken by Tōfuku-ji, which was founded in 1236, also in Kyōto. By means of this strategy, the antagonism of the influential older temples of the Tendai and Shingon sects was mollified, and the goodwill of the imperial court secured. Both Kennin-ji and Tōfuku-ji remain two of the leading Zen Buddhist temples in Japan, but none of their original buildings – or gardens – has survived.

Towards the end of the thirteenth century, Zen Buddhism was finally able to count a former emperor among its adherents. Kameyama had abdicated in 1274 at the young age of twenty-four, but as a former emperor who retains political power he had assumed the title of *Jōkō*, and he continued to govern over the imperial court. His influence, however, was whittled away through the machinations of the Kamakura shogunate. Faced with ever-increasing disappointments, Kameyama became a Buddhist monk in 1289. He was a devoted follower of Mukan Fumon, the third abbot of Tōfuku-ji, and when, in 1291, he decided to turn one of his two favourite residences into a Zen Buddhist temple, he invited Mukan Fumon to serve as the new temple's first abbot.

This temple became Nanzen-ji. It was situated near the Higashiyama mountain range, which forms the east flank of the city of Kyōto. Kameyama's original imperial villa was built on two levels, and the principal buildings of the new temple were constructed on the site where the main palace complex had stood. Kameyama, however, had his own private quarters on the hillside overlooking the rest of the palace grounds, and this became Nanzen-in, a smaller temple within the main temple. Nanzen-in retained the pond garden, which had been part of Kameyama's original private residence.

This beautiful garden had been planted with cherry trees from Yoshino and maples from Tatsuta, both regions in modern Nara prefecture, which had been the location of the imperial court before it moved to Kyōto. Pine trees had been

The turtle island in Nanzen-in's south garden is realistically represented by a semi-upright stone, which suggests a turtle's raised head, while clipped azaleas form its carapace.

brought from Sumiyoshi and reeds from Namba, both of which were sea ports on Ōsaka Bay. The pond was stocked with special small river frogs from Ide, which were particularly famous for their melancholy night-calls. All of these were well-established subject matter for poetry, and reflect how important literary associations were when designing aristocratic gardens of the period.

Kameyama continued to live at Nanzen-in until his death, in 1305. Afterwards, it was used as the private residence of the abbots of Nanzen-ji, but it burnt down in 1467, with the outbreak of the devastating civil war known as the Ōnin War. Most of Nanzen-ji itself was destroyed in that conflict, and work on reviving the great temple commenced in earnest only at the beginning of the seventeenth century. Nanzen-in's restoration did not start until the end of that century. As the site was being prepared for the construction of a new *hōjō* (abbot's hall), workers uncovered the ruins of Nanzen-in's former garden, and it was reconstructed as the south *hōjō* garden.

Buddhist symbolism came to be superimposed on various aspects of this garden. The pond, for example, was said to be in the shape of a coiled dragon – dragons being considered guardians of Buddhist teaching. The pond also acquired the name Sōgen-chi, which referred to the Chinese Zen master Dàjiàn

Huìnéng (Daikan Enō in Japanese), who died in 713. It is from Dàjiàn Huìnéng that all existent schools of Chinese and Japanese Zen Buddhism claim descent. Sōgen means the 'well-spring of Sōkei' – Sōkei being the Japanese pronunciation of Cáoxī, the location of Huìnéng's last temple: therefore, the image of this spring symbolises the idea that true Zen Buddhism is derived from one source, that is to say, Huìnéng. The south garden was, moreover, complemented by the creation of a new main garden for the *hōjō* on its west side, featuring a broadly 'U'-shaped pond representing the Chinese ideogram for 'heart'.

Kameyama's palace garden was thus transformed into a Zen temple garden, but more in terms of perception rather than through structural alterations. His original garden had been a landscape one with a pond and a waterfall, and this did not change. Since gardens were first built in Japan, their design has concentrated on creating a landscape, with hillocks representing mountains, and a body of water representing a stream, river, pond, lake or the sea itself. Even when stone and gravel became predominant features in gardens, the landscape remained the central concept behind the garden design. The idea of landscape is crucial to the understanding of Japanese gardens of all periods and all styles.

LEFT A superb aerial view of Tenju-an's east *hōjō* garden can be enjoyed from the balcony surrounding the top floor of Nanzen-ji's *sanmon* (main inner gateway).

RIGHT A path of geometrically set paving stones leads from Tenju-an's main gate to its *hōjō* (top left); detail of the *hōjō*'s east garden (centre left); Tenju-an's *shoin* (reception hall) opens on to the temple's south garden (bottom left); the south-garden pond dates from the fourteenth century (bottom right); a bridge in the style of *tanzaku* (strips of paper used for inscribing poems) spans a section of the south-garden pond (top right).

TENJU-AN SUB-TEMPLE, NANZEN-JI

Tenju-an was founded as a *tacchū* (sub-temple) of Nanzen-ji during the 1330s in honour of Mukan Fumon, Nanzen-ji's first abbot. It burnt down in the Ōnin War during the second half of the fifteenth century, and remained neglected until 1602, when work began on a new *hōjō* (abbot's hall). Tenju-an possesses two gardens: a landscape one with a double pond occupying the south half of its grounds; and a dry garden in front of the *hōjō*. The former retains the layout of a late-fourteenth/early-fifteenth-century pond garden, although sections of it were extensively remodelled at the beginning of the seventeenth century and again between 1904 and 1905. The dry garden features a path of square stepping stones set corner to corner, leading from Tenju-an's main gate up to the *hōjō*. Although these stepping stones are sometimes described as dating from the fourteenth century, their geometrical design is much more characteristic of garden styles of the seventeenth century. Another set of stepping stones leads from the *hōjō* to a cemetery among a grove of trees, where there is a memorial to Hosokawa Yūsai, who helped to restore Tenju-an in 1602. The rest of this dry garden was created by the garden architect Nakane Kinsaku in 1963.

THE TRADITION OF THE LANDSCAPE GARDEN IN JAPAN

The earliest Japanese gardens appeared during the fifth and sixth centuries. They were designed under the influence of Chinese culture and were constructed using a great deal of engineering expertise from China and Korea. The Chinese already had an ancient tradition of landscape gardens. One of the most important sets of imagery to influence the design of their gardens came from the Daoist legend of the Islands of the Immortals. (Daoism was a loosely knit but nonetheless complex system of philosophical and religious beliefs that had originated in China.) These fabled islands were supposed to exist somewhere off the north-east coast of China. Originally five in number, two were said to have been washed away in a great tidal wave, leaving just Mt Pénglái (known as Mt Hōrai in Japanese), Fāngzhàng (Hōjō) and Yíngzhōu (Eishū). These remote mountainous islands were believed to be the home of Daoist sages who had not only achieved immortality but were also in possession of the secret of never growing old. The tradition of representing these islands in a garden arose in China sometime during the Qin and Han dynasties, that is, between the third century BC and the third century AD. Practically speaking, inclusion of these islands entailed the construction of elaborate garden ponds ornamented with miniature islands.

When these Daoist beliefs were introduced to Japan, the image of small rugged islands scattered over the face of the ocean proved especially potent for the locals, who had a strong sense of being island-dwellers. The mystical islands of the Chinese mapped directly on to their cherished image of their own country. Even though the Chinese had their own famous mountains and lakes that were culturally important to them, the mystical Islands of the Immortals very much remained an imaginary realm for them. The Japanese, on the other hand, were very soon embellishing their representations of the islands with naturalistic touches evocative of their own coastal scenery. Islands

in the pond – whether they were large enough for a couple of pine trees, or nothing more than a single craggy boulder – became such a central feature of Japanese gardens that, by the seventh century, the Japanese word for island, *shima*, was being used to designate the entire landscaped garden.

Large stones were essential for establishing the outlines of the garden landscape. But this was not their sole purpose. Individual stones were chosen specifically as objects of aesthetic appeal. The Chinese had their own long tradition of stone appreciation, and this contributed considerably to the development of Japanese tastes. But the influence of Shintoism cannot be discounted, for mountain worship had always been an aspect of the Japanese native religion, and certain stones and boulders were considered to be divine.

In 794, the imperial capital was moved to what is now Kyōto. The location of the new capital lay between two rivers in a basin flanked by mountain ranges to its east, north and west. The water supply there was much more plentiful than at any other previous imperial capital. In gardening terms, this opened up the possibility of creating ponds on a larger scale than ever before. The surrounding mountains and local riverbeds, moreover, yielded different kinds of high-quality, naturally shaped stones, which were ideal for use in the garden. This included the fine white marble gravel from the river Shirakawa that became such a distinctive feature of Japanese gardens.

During the tenth century, a specifically Japanese style of palace architecture evolved, one in which the garden played an integral role. The style, known as *shinden-zukuri*, involved a complex of buildings at the centre of which was a main wide hall called the *shinden*, which faced south on to open ground laid with fine white Shirakawa river gravel. This open space was reserved for ceremonies, primarily the formal welcoming of guests to the palace. The Japanese word *niwa*, which is now translated as 'garden', originally referred to such flat open ground, although by the eleventh century it was also being applied to planted-up areas around buildings. Beyond the gravelled *niwa* was a landscape garden

An ancient sacred stone in the Saihō-ji garden is marked with a Shinto *shime-nawa* (tasselled rope of braided rice straw). A local deity, the Matsuo Myōjin, is said to have descended on this stone. When incorporated into a garden, stones such as these are known as *yōgō-seki*.

White gravel, symbolising purity, separates the *hōjō* (abbot's hall) at Tenryū-ji from its pond garden. This expanse of gravel, which accentuates the feeling of open space, is also reminiscent of the gravelled area that traditionally fronted the *shinden* (main hall) of tenth- and eleventh-century aristocratic palaces.

that featured a lake with islands linked by bridges. The lake was used for pleasure boating. It was fed by a stream, which ideally entered the garden from the east – this, it was believed, would wash away pestilence and evil influences from the premises. The terrain along the banks of the stream was varied with undulating *nosuji* (knolls) planted with flowers and low-growing pines.

This *shinden-zukuri* style of landscape garden had a profound influence on an early style of Buddhist temple garden – the Jōdo (paradise) style. The Jōdo (Pure Land) sect of Buddhism had a special devotion to the Amida Buddha (Amitābha in Sanskrit), who was believed to preside over the Gokuraku Jōdo or Saihō Jōdo (Pure Land in the West), and devotees prayed that they would be reborn in this paradise so that they might achieve enlightenment through meditation under the Buddha's direct guidance. Particularly during the eleventh century, there was a widespread belief that the final era of the world was on hand, during which enlightenment would no longer be possible in this existence.

From the tenth century onwards, this longing for paradise had been expressed in the form of temple gardens designed in the image of the Amida Buddha's Jōdo paradise. In gardens of this type, the main hall dedicated to the Buddha was built facing a central pond, which represented the Shippō-

chi (Lake of the Seven Treasures), which was imagined to lie at the heart of Amida's paradise. The opposite shore of the temple pond was intended to symbolise the present world, and, when the sliding doors of the façade of the main hall were opened, worshippers could see and pray to the shining golden figure of the Amida Buddha across the lake.

Developments such as these led to the emergence of monks with specialist gardening expertise in at least one Kyōto temple, Ninna-ji, which had always enjoyed a very close association with the imperial family. These monks were known as *ishitatezō* or *ishidatezō* (stone-raising monks). So central were stones to the landscape gardens of the day that the term *ishi wo tateru* not only literally meant 'to raise a stone', but was also used more generally in the sense of creating a garden.

With the growing rise in the popularity of the Zen school of Buddhism, many Buddhist temples that over the centuries had become derelict for one reason or another were refounded as Zen temples. They included temples that had formerly belonged to the Jōdo sect, and a few of them already possessed paradise-style gardens. This was another route by which Zen Buddhist temples inherited many of the traditions of Japanese garden design.

SAIHŌ-JI (KOKE-DERA, THE MOSS TEMPLE)

The Zen Buddhist temple Saihō-ji is so famous for its moss that it is generally known as the Moss Temple. Located among the foothills of the mountains to the west of Kyōto, its garden is a pond garden with three islands linked with turf bridges. The entire area is given over to mixed woodland, with Japanese maples growing alongside stately conifers such as Japanese cedar (*Cryptomeria japonica*; *sugi* in Japanese) and Hinoki cypress (*Chamaecyparis obtusa*). The garden is kept meticulously free of undergrowth. The conifers have had their lower branches removed (as is the way in Japan), and the illusion of spaciousness created by the tall columns they form, and the gracious shade they cast on the moss below, helps to give the garden an aura of other-worldly tranquillity. Among these surroundings, it seems possible to regain one's serenity of mind and spirit. This seems the perfect place to seek the enlightenment that Zen Buddhism speaks of.

LEFT Over many centuries, moss has taken over the grounds of Saihō-ji, but this is not how this garden was originally designed to look. Like Rokuon-ji (Kinkaku-ji), Saihō-ji was intended to be in the image of the Amida Buddha's Jōdo paradise, and it featured a bright spacious elegant garden ornamented with standing stones and clipped trees.

RIGHT The southernmost island of the pond at Saihō-ji is called Kasumi-jima (Misty Island) or simply Naga-jima (Long Island). In Musō Soseki's day, it was covered with sparkling white gravel.

BELOW A temple gardener at Saihō-ji shoulders a bamboo pannier (left); a row of stepping stones in the moss (centre); a garden path winds along the east shore of the pond, past a teahouse built in 1928 to provide refreshment for visitors to the garden and named the Tanhoku-tei, after one of Musō's original buildings.

Saihō-ji

There are said to be more than a hundred species of moss at Saihō-ji, but when its garden was first laid out, in the fourteenth century, the islands in the middle of the garden pond were spread with sparkling white gravel and planted with pine trees. The temple was renowned for its seasonal pageantry of cherry blossoms in the springtime, followed by lotus flowers in the summer and the colour of its maples in the autumn. There was a boathouse, and outings on to the pond took place. The garden was very much designed to be appreciated from the water as well as from land.

The present-day appearance of this garden at Saihō-ji is due more to chance than deliberate design. In 1339, the Japanese monk Musō Soseki founded Saihō-ji as a Rinzai Zen temple on the site of two late-twelfth-century Buddhist temples that had belonged to the Jōdo sect. One of these temples already had a pond garden in the Jōdo (paradise) style. Musō appears to have retained (or restored) many of the features of this garden, while adding a set of elegant new buildings. In contrast to the way the garden looks today, Musō's garden is said to have been full of brilliant sunlight. A section of the pond was spanned by a broad arched bridge from which it was possible to gaze down on a beautiful, two-storey pavilion, the upper storey of which was dedicated to a crystal reliquary containing Gautama Buddha's ashes. Musō named the pond Ōgon-chi (Golden Pond), after a description of paradise found in the *Hekigan-roku* (*The Blue Cliff Record*, or *Bìyán Lù* in Chinese), a twelfth-century Chinese collection of a hundred *kōan* (short anecdotes and sayings aimed at stimulating meditation). A smaller pond was called the Kongō-chi (Diamond Pond) after the Diamond Sutra.

But Saihō-ji suffered a steady decline of its fortunes over the subsequent centuries. It was badly damaged in the second half of the fifteenth century during the Ōnin War. The site was prone to flooding, having not only the garden's ponds but also three wellsprings and a small river in its immediate vicinity.

OPPOSITE TOP A rill formerly fed Saihō-ji's temple pond from the south-west. The temple's *yōgō-seki* (sacred stone) is in the foreground; it is festooned with rope, symbolising its divine associations.

OPPOSITE BOTTOM Clusters of stones in Saihō-ji's pond symbolise the auspicious crane and its companion, the turtle. Here, the boulders representing the crane can be seen beyond a bridge linking the southernmost of the pond's three main islands to the shore.

BELOW Plan of the gardens at Saihō-ji in their current form.

SAIHŌ-JI GARDEN

KEY

A = Probable site of Musō Soseki's pavilion
B = Probable site of Musō Soseki's bridge
C = Probable site of the Sairai-dō, which had been the Amida hall before Musō Soseki refounded the temple

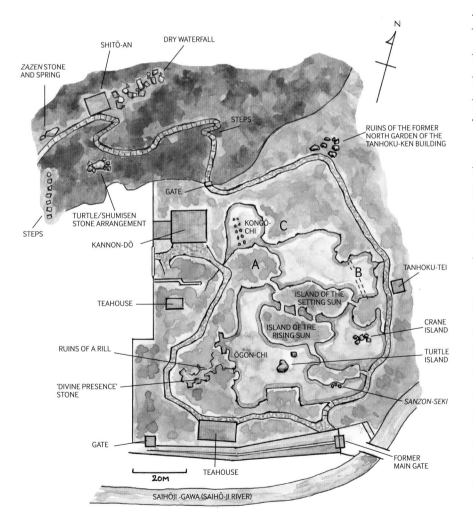

- SHITŌ-AN
- DRY WATERFALL
- *ZAZEN* STONE AND SPRING
- STEPS
- RUINS OF THE FORMER NORTH GARDEN OF THE TANHOKU-KEN BUILDING
- GATE
- TURTLE/SHUMISEN STONE ARRANGEMENT
- STEPS
- KANNON-DŌ
- KONGŌ-CHI
- C
- A
- TANHOKU-TEI
- TEAHOUSE
- ISLAND OF THE SETTING SUN
- B
- CRANE ISLAND
- ISLAND OF THE RISING SUN
- TURTLE ISLAND
- RUINS OF A RILL
- ŌGON-CHI
- 'DIVINE PRESENCE' STONE
- *SANZON-SEKI*
- GATE
- FORMER MAIN GATE
- 20M
- TEAHOUSE
- SAIHŌJI-GAWA (SAIHŌ-JI RIVER)

The oldest of the present temple buildings – a teahouse called the Shō'nan-tei – dates only from the beginning of the seventeenth century. By the beginning of the nineteenth century, the temple had become neglected, and moss had taken over the garden. It was then that the moss itself became the object of admiration.

This, however, is not the entire story. Musō built himself a hermitage for *zazen* (sitting meditation) on the slope overlooking the main temple garden. The site he chose is believed to have been the location of the second of the two twelfth-century temples, which had once stood there. While the original lower temple had been conceived in the image of the Amida Buddha's paradise, the temple on the slope was called Edo-ji – Edo, in this context, meaning the 'Defiled Land' and hence signifying the present world.

There was a cultural precedent for choosing a secluded spot in the wilderness for practising *zazen*. Bodhidharma, the Indian monk who is supposed to have introduced Chán Buddhism to China, was said to have meditated in a cave for nine consecutive years, his face turned to the wall. Also, the persecution of Buddhist temples in ninth-century China forced many Chán monks to abandon the cities and find refuge in remoter areas of the Chinese empire.

Musō named his own hermitage Shitō-an (Hermitage which Points to the East) after a legend associated with Ryō-zasu, a Chinese Chán Buddhist monk of the eighth century. Ryō-zasu is said to have realised the futility of seeking scholarly knowledge after he had an encounter with the Chán master Baso Dō'itsu (Mǎzǔ Dàoyī in Chinese). He gave up the school in which he had been teaching his many disciples and disappeared up a mountain. Several centuries later, a man came across an ancient monk sitting in meditation on a rock. When he asked the monk whether he might be Ryō-zasu, the monk merely raised his hand and pointed eastwards. While the man was looking in the direction in which he was pointing, the monk vanished.

Musō's Shitō-an, as its name suggested, faced east. It looked out on to a garden built along the slope of the hillside. The building has been heavily

LEFT Shallow steps lead up to boulders shielding a spring – now sadly dry. On the right, there is a flat-topped monolith traditionally known as Musō Soseki's *zazen* (sitting meditation) stone.

OPPOSITE The path up the mountainside leads to the Shitō-an (top left); the Shitō-an, which faces east, looks out on to these stones (right), thought to constitute one of the earliest surviving examples in Japan of a *kare-taki* (dry waterfall) – it is left to the imagination of the beholder to feel the force of the rushing water; a flight of stone steps connects the upper garden with the rest of the temple (bottom left).

restored, indeed rebuilt, over the centuries, and the current building dates only from 1878, although it retains some ancient pieces of timber. It looks out on to a cluster of massive boulders set deeply into a groove in the side of the hill, like a yawning mouth. There are many more, slightly smaller boulders, stones and rocks, all looking as though they have tumbled down the slope, and come to rest in clusters wherever the ground has slightly levelled off. Most garden historians agree that these boulders are meant to represent a three-tiered waterfall, terminating by the foot of the Shitō-an itself in a series of cascades composed of smaller stones.

Not everybody, however, agrees with this interpretation. For one thing, the arrangement does not obviously look like a waterfall. The imaginary water course is not clearly defined, nor are there any signs of pebbles or smooth stones having been laid out to suggest a stream bed. Indeed, the eminent twentieth-century garden architect Nakane Kinsaku noted that he had not been able to find any account written before the sixteenth century that described these boulders as a dry waterfall arrangement. He controversially argued that this was not a waterfall at all, but the ruins of a series of steep stone steps, which led up the mountainside – possibly to a gazebo, which Musō is known to have

had constructed high on the slope. Another important garden historian and designer, Shigemori Mirei, concurred. For his part, he hypothesised that the stones had been part of a garden adjoining the twelfth-century temple that had formerly stood there. An eleventh-century garden design manual known as the *Sakutei-ki*, which is believed to have been produced by the aristocratic court official and poet Tachibana no Toshitsuna, described the use of stones along a slope in order to produce the impression of a ruinous eroded terrain. The manual, moreover, applied the term *kare-sansui* to this method of laying stones. Shigemori felt that this might have been intended at Saihō-ji.

Disagreements of this kind reflect the difficulty of interpreting ancient gardens. Much concerning early Zen temple gardens remains obscure, as there is no surviving documentation. Musō himself is a tantalisingly remote character. That he had a love of gardens is attested by his contemporaries, and Musō himself in one of his writings mentioned a garden he created at Sanne-in, a part of Rinsen-ji, a temple in Kyōto to which he was appointed abbot by the emperor Go-Daigo in 1333 or 1335. Sadly this garden has not survived. Musō Soseki is frequently described as one of Japan's most influential early garden designers, yet few facts are known about his gardening activities.

LEFT The wide veranda of Tenryū-ji's *shoin* (reception hall), located on the north side of the temple pond, provides a sweeping view of the garden and the picturesque mountainside of Arashiyama.

RIGHT The moss-mottled, bottle-shaped stone halfway up the waterfall represents a carp attempting to climb the falls. The stone footbridge, which crosses in front of the waterfall, is the earliest example of its type in Japan and served as an important model.

TENRYŪ-JI

Musō Soseki, who died in 1351 at the age of seventy-five, had a career of two halves. As a young man, he led a peripatetic life, moving from temple to temple, and from one hermitage to another, all the while gaining a considerable reputation as a Zen monk. At the age of fifty, he came to the notice of the emperor Go-Daigo, who invited him to become the abbot of Nanzen-ji in Kyōto, a great honour indeed for a Buddhist priest who had hitherto spent most his time travelling around the provinces. Thereafter, Musō attracted the patronage of the leaders of the Kamakura shogunate. The shogunate, however, was in the grip of a power struggle with Go-Daigo, and after one of its chief military commanders – Ashikaga Taka'uji – defected to the imperial side, it finally collapsed in 1333. Go-Daigo assumed the reins of power, and under his patronage Musō returned to Kyōto to serve as the abbot of Rinsen-ji and, for a while, of Nanzen-ji once again.

Taka'uji then rebelled against the emperor, who in 1336 was forced to abdicate in favour of an imperial prince who was backed by Taka'uji. Taka'uji became the *de facto* ruler of Japan, and two years later he was appointed shogun. Meanwhile, Go-Daigo fled to the Yoshino mountain range in south

Nara and set up a rival imperial court to the one in Kyōto. Remarkably, Musō managed to survive all of these turbulent regime changes.

In autumn 1339, Go-Daigo died, and the new shogun and his brother, Tadayoshi, decided that a new temple should be built to placate the soul of the former emperor, whom they had effectively deposed. Musō was invited to become its first abbot. The location for the new temple was the imperial villa Kameyama-dono, where Go-Daigo had spent his childhood. Kameyama-dono had been the other favourite residence of the emperor Kameyama, who founded Nanzen-ji, and it is believed that prior to that it had been the site of Japan's first Zen Buddhist temple Danrin-ji, built in the ninth century on the orders of an empress.

The new temple, Tenryū-ji, was finally inaugurated in 1345. Since then, Tenryū-ji has been ravaged by fire eight times, and the present-day *hōjō* (abbot's hall) was built only in 1899. But its landscape garden is believed to date back to the fourteenth century, and it has traditionally been attributed to Musō. This superb pond garden sits at the foot of Ogura-yama, a mountain also known by its ancient nickname Kame-yama. It is highly likely that the imperial villa had a pond, but, without doubt, this has been much altered.

A tree-covered *tsukiyama* (man-made hillock) rises from the water's edge on the farther side of the pond, and into the side of this hillock has been set a striking, three-tiered cascade delineated by a course of massive boulders. Halfway up this waterfall, there is a stone that resembles the raised head of a carp facing determinedly upstream, its powerful back hoary with lichen. It is an example of a waterfall style known as *ryūmon-baku* (dragon-gate), in which the carp symbolises perseverance in the pursuit of enlightenment. A simple bridge consisting of three slabs of natural stone crosses the plunge pool at the bottom of the waterfall. Clustered boulders in the water near the waterfall represent rocky islets.

Although individual details are difficult to see from the *hōjō* (abbot's hall), it is only from this side of the pond that the composition of the garden can be fully appreciated – for what is represented here is a vast landscape in miniature. The waterfall is meant to look like a spectacular natural formation seen from a great distance. The carefully positioned islets in front of it and the narrow spits of land tipped with boulders, which jut sharply into the pond from the foreshore, are intended to imitate a rough coastal seascape with jagged headlands. All contribute to the illusion of a landscape receding farther and farther into the

distance. This feeling of depth is accentuated by the presence of a diminutive triangular stone just above the waterfall arrangement. This stone is not part of the waterfall design itself, but is meant to suggest a mountain behind the waterfall. Stones such as this, known as *enzan-seki* (distant-mountain stone), came to be frequently employed in the design of dry waterfalls.

The overall effect of the composition is like that of a Chinese ink brush landscape painting, in which the minimum is depicted in order to create the greatest feeling of depth and distance. Mountains, waterfalls and bridges were all familiar subject matter for such paintings. It is known that the shogun Ashikaga Taka'uji sent a trading ship to China in 1342 expressly to raise funds for building Tenryū-ji. This vessel would have brought back many items of Chinese manufacture, including examples of the exquisite workmanship and artistry in ceramics, carvings, published books, bronzes and paintings, which the cognoscenti in Japan – Buddhist monks, aristocrats and high-ranking *bushi* (members of the military class) – all craved to possess.

Musō Soseki had just taken over at Saihō-ji when he was appointed abbot of Tenryū-ji, and if he was indeed involved in the planning of the gardens at both of these temples he would have undertaken the work more or less

BELOW LEFT Tenryū-ji's garden pond, called the Sōgen-chi, shares its name with the garden pond at Nanzen-in.

BELOW RIGHT The blue silhouette of the peak of Atago-yama in the distance provides the backdrop to the north section of Tenryū-ji's pond garden.

simultaneously. But the waterfalls (if the clusters of stones on the hillside above Saihō-ji can be considered to be one) are so different in both scale and style that some historians have questioned whether they could have been designed by the same person. One theory is that the garden at Tenryū-ji was created not by somebody like Musō but by a Chinese gardener, who was perhaps also a Buddhist monk – someone who, in any case, had deep, first-hand knowledge of Chinese artistic methods.

The truth is lost in the mists of history. Musō himself remains an enigmatic figure. On the one hand, he is portrayed in legend as an ascetic who longed for nothing more than solitude. But then there is the Musō who retained the favour of Japan's rulers through innumerable political upheavals. Was this because his unworldliness, charisma or spirituality won him the esteem of the most ruthless and powerful men in society – or because he was a consummate courtier who shared the elegant tastes of the aristocracy and was adept at

manipulating political favour? Was he fashionable because he offered the ruling classes a palatable form of Zen Buddhism that was less stringent than the original teachings of the Chinese schools?

A monk who was a contemporary of Musō's wrote critically of him, suggesting that he preferred gardens to meditation. Musō's own views about gardens are reflected in a brief passage in *Muchū mondōshū* (1342), a collection of religious discourses in the form of dialogues between himself and the shogun's brother, Ashikaga Tadayoshi. He observed that, when a Buddhist looks out on to a garden, he realises that no matter how transient all things are, everything is interconnected because they all partake in *busshō* (Buddha-nature), the potential for all things to attain nirvana, that is, spiritual salvation. But Musō warned that the pursuit of perfection in a particular art form was not the same thing as striving after spiritual enlightenment. Nothing, not even the exhilaration of creating gardens, could serve as a substitute for meditation.

ROKUON-JI (KINKAKU-JI)

The garden at Rokuon-ji, or Kinkaku-ji as it is popularly known, was originally created by Ashikaga Yoshimitsu, a former shogun, for his villa the Kitayama-dono. Based on the Jōdo (paradise) style, it was a magnificent celebration of the blessedness of nirvana, and yet at the same time it was a glorification of his own worldly power and of the ascendancy of the Ashikaga dynasty. Many of the small islands in the pond, therefore, take the form of a crane or, more often, a turtle, both being Daoist symbols of longevity and good fortune.

There is also one particularly Zen Buddhist feature: a *ryūmon-baku* (dragon-gate waterfall) with a boulder representing a carp attempting to swim upstream. It is a symbol of perseverance, the indefatigable struggle of the spirit to attain enlightenment. Located a short distance to the rear of the Kinkaku (Golden Pavilion), it is now next to the paved path, which guides tourists around the garden, but originally it was meant to be viewed from a two-storey assembly hall called the Tenkyō-kaku, the top floor of which was connected to the first storey of the Kinkaku by a spectacular roofed walkway suspended over the lake.

OPPOSITE Rokuon-ji's temple pond is called the Kyōko-chi (Mirror Lake). According to Buddhist legend, Enma, the ruler of the underworld, possessed a mirror that reflects the true state of a person's soul.

CLOCKWISE FROM TOP LEFT This boat-shaped Japanese white pine (*Pinus parviflora*) at Rokuon-ji is said to have once been a favourite bonsai belonging to the former shogun Ashikaga Yoshimitsu; Rokuon-ji's famous *ryūmon-baku*

(dragon-gate waterfall) is distinguished by its characterful carp-stone situated at the foot of the falls (top right); another of Rokuon-ji's auspicious turtle-themed islands (below right); the Kinkaku looks out on to the pond (below left).

FORMER VILLAS OF THE ASHIKAGA SHŌGUN: ROKUON-JI AND JISHŌ-JI

Musō Soseki continued to be venerated as a great Zen master after his death in 1351. Among those who revered him was Taka'uji's grandson Yoshimitsu, the third shogun of the Ashikaga shogunate. Yoshimitsu made pilgrimages to Saihō-ji, where he is said to have spent time meditating in the Shitō-an, Musō's hermitage on the slope above the main temple buildings. When Yoshimitsu decided to build a splendid new villa for himself, he modelled much of it on Saihō-ji. Like Saihō-ji, Yoshimitsu's palatial villa, known as Kitayama-dono, featured a beautiful pavilion dedicated to a reliquary that contained Gautama Buddha's ashes; only his was three storeys high and was covered in gold leaf. After Yoshimitsu's death in 1408, the building was designated a Zen Buddhist temple in accordance with Yoshimitsu's will. The new temple was named Rokuon-ji, but it is familiarly referred to as Kinkaku-ji (Temple of the Golden Pavilion).

Yoshimitsu acquired the property in 1397. A grand villa complex had once stood there – the residence of the powerful, twelfth- to thirteenth-century aristocrat Fujiwara (later Saionji) Kintsune, who has also founded a Buddhist temple close by. Called Saionji (from which his descendants thereafter took their surname), this temple was dedicated to the Amida Buddha and had a handsome garden in the Jōdo (paradise) style. In 1394, Yoshimitsu abdicated as shogun in favour of his eight-year-old, eldest son, and in the following year he became a Buddhist monk. But far from relinquishing his hold on political power, Yoshimitsu used this move to consolidate his grip over both secular and religious society. His new palace was designed as a testimony to his supremacy.

In modelling his garden after the Jōdo style, Yoshimitsu was following the example of Saihō-ji, although it is unclear how much of Saionji Kintsune's original garden he kept. Yoshimitsu's new garden was designed principally to

LEFT A *sanzon-seki* (three sacred stones) arrangement, symbolising Buddha and his attendants, provides the focal point of the largest island, the Ashihara-jima, as seen from the Kinkaku (Golden Pavilion). A low stone in front of the central boulder is thought to represent the Buddha's lotus-shaped dais.

BELOW RIGHT The exquisite detail of the south-west shoreline of Rokuon-ji's garden pond is designed to be viewed by boat.

BOTTOM RIGHT A second *sanzon-seki* arrangement is situated along Ashihara-jima's south shore, while a third is on the island itself.

First built *c*.1398, the Kinkaku's top storey is thought to have been the only part of the structure originally decorated with gold leaf. The building was much modified between 1537 and 1538. In 1950, it was set alight by a junior Buddhist monk and burnt to the ground. Reconstructed five years later, it was regilded in 1987 with more than 200,000 sheets of gold leaf.

be viewed from the Kinkaku (Golden Pavilion), which looks out over a large pond with a long narrow central island. This island has the name Ashihara-jima – Ashihara (which translates as reed bed) being a mythological name for Japan. Modelled after the southernmost of the three islands in the garden at Saihō-ji, the Ashihara-jima has a shoreline set with imposing boulders, in the centre of which there is a three-stone grouping that is best viewed from the pavilion. There is another three-stone grouping on the other side of the island. Such arrangements are called *sanzon-seki* (three sacred stones) in Japanese because they were thought to be reminiscent of the way in which Buddhas are frequently depicted, flanked on either side by attendant bodhisattvas. The main arrangement on the Ashihara-jima at Kinkaku-ji is an adaptation of the example that can still be seen at Saihō-ji.

Ashikaga Yoshimitsu's descendants shared his enthusiasm for building magnificent palaces and gardens, none more so than his grandson Yoshimasa, who likewise built himself a splendid residence modelled on Musō Soseki's Saihō-ji. But while the Kitayama-dono symbolised Yoshimitsu's power at its zenith, Yoshimasa's Higashiyama-dono represented his withdrawal from political responsibilities into the realms of art and religion.

Yoshimasa was the eighth shogun of the Ashikaga dynasty. Thwarted in his attempt to curb the power of the influential but quarrelsome noble clans, which were beginning to challenge the dominance of the shogunate, he retreated into a life of pleasure, preferring to indulge his love of the arts rather than addressing the effects of a succession of severe famines and the poor state of the shogunate's finances. His inept handling of the question of his own successor exacerbated the climate of political instability, which

Many noble families contributed famous garden stones towards the creation of the garden at Rokuon-ji. Several still bear the name of their original donor: one such stone is the massive Akamatsu Stone, set as a single outcrop in the pond. It is the upright rectangular boulder in front of the stones on the left of the stone lantern.

erupted in 1467 into full-blown warfare within the city of Kyōto. This civil war, known as the Ōnin War, destroyed the administrative heart of the capital and eventually spread throughout the entire country. It was not until 1477 that its flames were finally extinguished. Meanwhile, Yoshimasa relinquished the title of shogun to his son in 1473.

He had already been planning a villa for himself, when the Ōnin War broke out, so he was forced to abort his plans. In 1482, Yoshimasa chose to start Higashiyama-dono on the site of a former temple located on the east fringe of the city. He moved there in 1483 in order to oversee construction work. When he died in 1490, the last of his buildings, the Kannon-den (Hall of the Kannon) was not quite completed. It is this building that is now known popularly as the Ginkaku (Silver Pavilion). The Ginkaku was never decorated in silver leaf, but painted in black lacquer, which faded to a silvery sheen, from which the building acquired its nickname only in the eighteenth century.

Yoshimasa modelled Higashiyama-dono more closely on Saihō-ji than even his grandfather Ashikaga Yoshimitsu had done with his Kitayama-dono. He also had the expertise of several garden specialists at his disposal. Being a great patron of the arts, Yoshimasa kept a host of retainers, each of whom was a master in one or another field of artistic expertise, whether it was Chinese art, the appreciation of rare incense, the tea ceremony, flower arrangement, poetry or garden design. These men were known collectively as *dōhōshū*. Many belonged to a sect of Buddhism, not of the Zen school, which attracted a large number of its followers from the bottom rungs of society. How some of them came by their specialist knowledge is not clear, although some families had worked for their Ashikaga masters for generations. One of the most famous among Yoshimasa's *dōhōshū* was Sōami, an expert on Chinese works of art, particularly ink-brush paintings, who had a reputation as an accomplished painter in his own right. Another of Yoshimasa's *dōhōshū* was the gardening master Zen'ami.

Zen'ami belonged to a stigmatised social class known as the *kawaramono* (riverbank dwellers), who had traditionally been involved in 'unclean' work, such as butchery and tanning, as well as the burial of dead bodies. They were also engaged in professions such as thatching, plastering, well-digging and pond dredging. By the fifteenth century, there were men of this social class who were expert at building gardens, especially with regard to the procurement, transport and setting of heavy garden stones and boulders. These garden experts came to be known as *senzui-kawaramono*. Zen'ami was not only a favourite of Yoshimasa's but had also previously enjoyed the patronage of his father, Yoshinori, the sixth shogun. Zen'ami would have been too old to work on the garden for Yoshimasa's Higashiyama-dono, but his son Koshirō and grandson Matashirō are known to have followed in his footsteps, and it is quite possible that they had a hand in its construction.

Zen'ami was admired for his expertise in building landscapes. He is said to have excelled at building both *tsukiyama* (man-made hillocks) and ponds, and was known for his superb eye when it came to the placement of standing stones and trees. Zen'ami appears to have had a gift for scaling down the aristocratic *shinden-zukuri* style of garden to fit a much more restricted space, but without making the result feel small or cramped. Quite to the contrary, an admirer of his wrote that, in one garden, Zen'ami had succeeded in producing the illusion of a grand vista, with mountain ranges fading behind mountain ranges far into the distant horizon.

Interestingly, Zen'ami is reported to have been knowledgable about *bonseki* and *bonsan*, both forms of miniature landscaping that had originated in China but had been taken up with great avidity in Japan. *Bonseki* involved the presentation of an exceptional, naturally shaped stone in a shallow bowl or pot filled with soil or fine gravel. In *bonsan*, the arrangement included miniaturised trees (what would today be called *bonsai*), and the stone would be intended to represent a mountain. In other instances, the miniature

The garden at Jishō-ji looks very much like it does today in this illustration from a 1799 guidebook to Kyōto entitled *Miyako Rinsen Meishō Zue*. The Kōgetsudai (Moon-Facing Mound), however, was not as high as it now is, and there is a rectangular flower bed in the middle of the raked Ginshadan. The Ginkaku (Silver Pavilion), can be seen to the right of the pond. Formerly known as the Kannon-den (Hall of the Kannon), this building acquired its nickname during the eighteenth century. Since then, the temple has been popularly referred to as Ginkaku-ji (Temple of the Silver Pavilion).

mountain would be created with fine gravel. Zen'ami's designs for the garden would no doubt have been honed by his awareness of the techniques of *bonseki* and *bonsan*. A shared interest in these art forms would also have helped familiarise his patrons with the idea of a landscape garden on a small scale – one which, importantly, used no running water. If a pond, waterfall, river or the sea needed to be represented, it could now be done symbolically with gravel, sand and stones.

Ashikaga Yoshimasa's villa became the Zen Buddhist temple Jishō-ji after his death, but it did not fare well and over the centuries it became rundown. Perhaps the biggest changes to its garden occurred after an extensive rebuilding programme was initiated in 1615, lasting over two decades. During this time, the lake is believed to have been reduced to about half its original size, and the Ginkaku (Silver Pavilion) as well as the one other surviving original building – the architecturally important Tōgu-dō – were moved to their current locations. A new *hōjō* (abbot's hall) was built alongside the Tōgu-dō, and at some point a dry gravel garden was created in front of this building, filling the erratically shaped space between it and the surviving portion of pond.

It is for this dry gravel garden that Jishō-ji is now celebrated, yet nobody knows exactly when it was built or by whom. The only certain thing is that this garden did not exist in Yoshimasa's day, and that it was created after 1615. The dry gravel garden is composed of two striking features: the Ginshadan, a large, irregularly shaped raised bed with a pattern of alternating columns of levelled gravel and of gravel raked into stripes; and the flat-topped, conical mound called the Kōgetsudai (Moon-Facing Mound). The pattern of the Ginshadan (which can be translated as the 'Rough Sea of Silver Sand') suggests a wave motif – not a rolling surf but shallow, choppy waves – so that, together with the Kōgetsudai, it is possible to read the composition as an extremely schematic representation of a mountain-and-sea landscape. The use of raked gravel is characteristic of the *kare-sansui* (dry-landscape) style of the seventeenth

century, but the mound is unique. There is a long-standing legend that the white gravel used to create the Ginshadan and the Kōgetsudai was dredged out of Yoshimasa's pond when the garden was being restored, but the mound is not composed of white gravel throughout. It is shaped out of *masado*, otherwise known as *masa-tsuchi*, a type of local soil made up of decomposed granite and clay. The fine white gravel is mixed with water before being applied to the surface of the mound. Not only does this allow the gravel to adhere better to the *masado*, but it produces a smooth and even finish.

The Ginshadan and the Kōgetsudai have been said to represent a view of China's famous West Lake in Hanzhou, but the shape of the Kōgetsudai is more likely to remind Japanese visitors these days of that most iconic of Japanese mountains – Mt Fuji. An illustration of Jishō-ji's garden in a 1799 guidebook to Kyōto's gardens shows a rectangular flower bed within the Ginshadan and a much lower and flatter Kōgetsudai, which bears little resemblance to Mt Fuji. In the picture, the mound also has four concentric circles raked into its flat summit. Although there was an ancient tradition, particularly at Shinto shrines and Buddhist temples, of having a pair of gravel cones in the garden as symbols of purity, the 1799 illustration suggests that the Kōgetsudai was not initially conceived as a cone with its top cut off, but that it grew taller over the centuries, eventually coming to look more and more like Mt Fuji.

THE ARTIST-MONK SESSHŪ
AND THE JŌEI-JI GARDEN

Ashikaga Yoshimasa was a great collector of fine Chinese art. Pieces from his collection were used to decorate the rooms of his villa for his cultural gatherings, at which guests would compose poetry, enjoy the scent of rare incense or share a sip of tea. The cultivation of fine sensibilities, especially through the practice of calligraphy and ink-brush painting, as well as poetry composition, was similarly very much part of the intellectual life of Rinzai Zen temples in the capital Kyōto.

Zen monks assiduously maintained a cult of amateurism, so as not to allow these activities to become a major preoccupation. Zen Buddhism, after all, taught the importance of 'letting go', of freeing oneself not only from specific spiritually corrupting tendencies such as cupidity, pride and envy but also, more generally, from desire itself. Nonetheless, by the second half of the fourteenth century, there were Zen monks who were professional artists. Many of these monks were at Shōkoku-ji, a major Rinzai Zen Buddhist temple in Kyōto founded by Ashikaga Yoshimitsu in 1382. These monks provided instruction in art, as well as religious guidance, to their disciples. The subject matter of these artist–monks was not restricted to specifically Buddhist themes, as it encompassed flowers, birds, animals and especially landscapes.

The most famous of all the artists to emerge from Shōkoku-ji was Sesshū, who is known particularly for his landscape paintings. It is perhaps not surprising, therefore, that his name has been linked in one way or another with nearly forty gardens. Born in 1420 in the west province of Bichū (modern-day Okayama prefecture), Sesshū became a novice monk at the age of ten. At some stage he moved to Kyōto and joined Shōkoku-ji, where he studied ink-brush painting with a monk of the temple, Tenshō Shūbun, who was an important landscape artist as well as a sculptor. In his late thirties or early forties, Sesshū moved to the land of Suō (now the south-east region of Yamaguchi prefecture at the

very west tip of the main Japanese island of Honshū) in the hope of finding a passage to China. In 1467, after a lengthy wait, Sesshū was given a berth on a ship sponsored by the lord of Suō. After spending two years in China studying the latest painting techniques and travelling widely, he returned to Japan. He led a mainly itinerant life for the next fifteen or so years and eventually settled in Suō at the age of sixty-five. He died c.1506.

Sesshū has traditionally been connected with the distinguished garden found at Jōei-ji, a Rinzai Zen temple in the tiny city of Yamaguchi. This city was the stronghold of the Ōuchi clan, who ruled the land of Suō, and Sesshū is said to have designed the garden at the request of Ōuchi Masahiro, lord of Suō, not long after his return from China. Built into a kind of natural amphitheatre created by the tall hill on to which the temple backs, the garden has three sections of very differing characteristics. The front part is in the *kare-sansui* (dry-landscape) style. Beyond this, there is a pond garden with small islands. Lastly, the slopes surrounding the garden are densely forested with maples, conifers and bamboos, which produce an effect akin to drapery around the back of a circular open stage.

It is the *kare-sansui* section of Jōei-ji's garden that makes the viewer think of an ink-brush painting of a vast mountain landscape. The ground gently undulates; tucked in among its folds or perched on the top of a rise are clusters of lustrous stones, interspersed with a few closely pruned azaleas. There are no other shrubs, let alone trees. Most unusually for an old garden, the garden is grassed over rather than gravelled or covered in moss. The eye is led across the landscape from one group of stones to the next – just as in a classical ink brush landscape painting, the eye travels from mountain range to mountain range as they recede into the misty distance.

Although there are no extant records proving Sesshū had a hand in creating any part of this garden, the bold dynamic way in which these stones have been arranged bears a powerful similarity to Sesshū's style of ink brush landscape painting. The choice of stone is also very distinctive.

Sesshū is famous for his bold stokes of the brush and for his decisive forceful style. The mountains in his painting are often jagged, as though they have just pushed their way out of the ground or perhaps split along a fault line. Similarly, the stones in the *kare-sansui* (dry-landscape) section of the Jōei-ji garden are not rounded but strikingly angular, with flat surfaces, ridges and sharp edges. Dark in colour and coarse-grained, they are flecked with feldspar, which gives them a streaky aged appearance. Lichen has added further mottling, which brings to mind the way in which gradations of black and grey are used in ink-brush paintings to represent deep ravines and overhanging cliffs.

Many of the groupings of stones have had the names of famous Chinese mountains attributed to them, reflecting Sesshū's sojourn in that country. But among them all, there is a lone triangular stone with sloping sides, which unmistakably

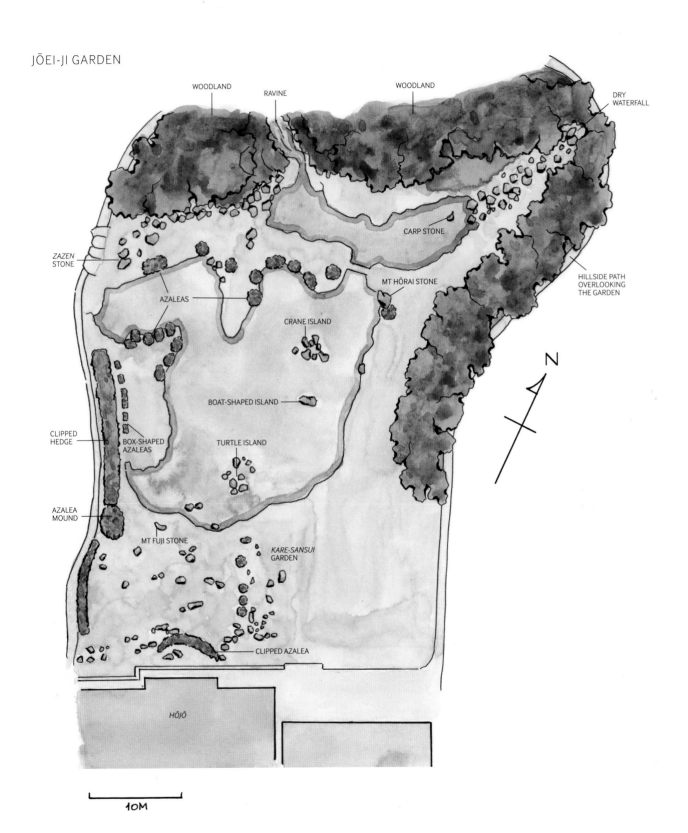

JŌEI-JI GARDEN

WOODLAND
RAVINE
WOODLAND
DRY WATERFALL
CARP STONE
ZAZEN STONE
HILLSIDE PATH OVERLOOKING THE GARDEN
MT HŌRAI STONE
AZALEAS
CRANE ISLAND
BOAT-SHAPED ISLAND
CLIPPED HEDGE
BOX-SHAPED AZALEAS
TURTLE ISLAND
AZALEA MOUND
MT FUJI STONE
KARE-SANSUI GARDEN
CLIPPED AZALEA
HŌJŌ

10M

resembles the flanks of Mt Fuji. Until recently, this stone was covered by a carefully cropped azalea that made it look even more like Mt Fuji, with the exposed tip of the stone suggesting the mountain's familiar, snow-capped summit. The presence of Mt Fuji among a miniature landscape reminiscent of Chinese ink-brush paintings is significant: here is a unified cosmos, which incorporates the cultures of both Japan and China.

The other parts of the garden show an extremely skilled and assured hand, but are of a rather different character. The large, irregularly shaped pond beyond the *kare-sansui* (dry-landscape) lawn has small islands, which take their theme from familiar Daoist imagery, such as the auspicious turtle and the crane — symbols of longevity. Still farther to the back, a bank of boulders has been set into the hillside skirting the garden. These stones help to add a feeling of ruggedness to the garden in the manner recommended in the earliest surviving Japanese garden manual — the *Sakutei-ki*. In a cleft in the hillside in the north-east corner of the garden, there is also a tremendous dry waterfall.

The choice and positioning of the large stones around the pond and along the mountain slope are masterly, and they probably reflect the advanced technical expertise that had developed in a major cultural centre such as Kyōto. Perhaps Sesshū collaborated with gardening experts such as *senzui-kawaramono*, who like Sesshū himself had come here from the capital. The truth will probably never be known.

THE SUB-TEMPLES OF KYŌTO AND THEIR GARDENS

As the influence of landscape painting on garden design continued to grow in the capital Kyōto, more and more smaller-sized gardens were built. This was especially so in and around the city's major Buddhist temples, which saw a burgeoning of smaller institutions emerging under their protective umbrellas. Prominent temples of the Rinzai Zen school all had clusters of *tacchū* (sub-temples), which competed for space within the grounds of the temple complex.

Modelled on a Chinese monastic tradition, the first *tacchū* in Japan were mausoleums of revered Zen masters, which were maintained by their disciples. Later on, the term came to be applied to hermitages, which senior monks would establish after their retirement from their duties within the main temple. There,

they would gather their own disciples around them. *Tacchū* enjoyed a semi-autonomous status, usually having their own groups of financial backers and worshippers. Physically, however, they were located within the grounds of the mother temple, and the amount of land that was available to each was limited.

The fires of the Ōnin War wiped out nearly all of the major temples in the capital, along with their innumerable sub-temples. No *tacchū* garden has survived from before this civil war. The earliest extant examples date from the middle of the sixteenth century, when temples were being reconstructed and new sub-temples founded. One of these is the tiny gem of a garden at Reiun-in, a sub-temple of Myōshin-ji. Occupying a narrow rectangular space, no more than 10m/33ft long and 3.5m/12ft wide, wedged between a temple building

and a high plastered earthen wall, the garden comprises about a dozen exquisite stones and fine gravel and depicts a truly panoramic scene of mountains, a rocky gorge, cascades and a wide lake with a range of hills in the background. The way the garden design flows seamlessly from a mountain view to a lake scene makes it seem like a scroll painting that is being unrolled before one's eyes. This garden has been historically attributed to the Zen Buddhist artist–monk Shiken Seidō, who, like Sesshū, originally was at Shōkoku-ji.

Another early surviving example of a *tacchū* (sub-temple) garden is found at Daisen-in, a sub-temple belonging to Daitoku-ji, also in Kyōto. This garden encompasses all four sides of Daisen-in's *hōjō* (abbot's hall). The *hōjō* was an innovation of Zen Buddhist temples, and it played a central role in the life of

the temple community. This was where the abbot lived, worked and taught. The building was a symbol of his authority. Each sub-temple had its own *hōjō*, while there was a separate *hōjō* for the main temple.

The basic layout of the *hōjō* involved six rooms. The three facing south were the public rooms. The central room was the *shicchū*, where prayers were offered and religious ceremonies conducted. To the rear of the *shicchū*, there was the *butsu-ma* (shrine room), dedicated to the Buddha or to the founding abbot of the temple. A reception room flanked the *shicchū* on either side. The rooms around the back of the building were more private in nature. Sometimes, a narrow room was squeezed in behind the *butsu-ma*: this served the abbot as his dormitory. The room occupying the north-east corner of the *hōjō* (abbot's

OPPOSITE The Kannon and Fudō stones dominate the north-east corner of Daisen-in's *hōjō* garden. On their right, an intricate mountain cascade has been created using much smaller stones so as to add a feeling of further depth to the garden. The triangular stone to the right of the stone bridge represents a crane's wing and the flat rock in front of it symbolises its tail.

BELOW This garden deftly manipulates the viewer's sense of distance, and needs to be enjoyed from a sitting position for its panoramic effect to be fully appreciated.

hall) was usually the abbot's *shoin* (study), where he might meet his personal guests.

The heart of the Daisen-in *hōjō* garden faces the *shoin*, not the public rooms. Two immense standing stones are positioned in front of tall ancient camellias, pruned to represent a range of mountains. The stone on the right is identified with the Kannon Bosatsu (the bodhisattva Avalokiteśvara), and the other with the Buddhist guardian divinity Fudō-myō'ō (Acalanātha in Sanskrit), although some accounts of the garden describe the stones the other way around. On the raised ground to the right of the two stones, there is a dry waterfall, capped at the very back by a round-topped *enzan-seki* (distant-mountain stone), suggesting the presence of a mountain rearing up in the far distance behind the waterfall. The rippled stone in front of the *enzan-seki* represents falling water.

Two further sets of cascades, with fine white gravel denoting the current, flow down in front of the Kannon and Fudō stones. Here the current divides. One branch runs along the north side of the *hōjō*, winding its way around a collection of stones representing a turtle. It then proceeds under a corridor that leads from the *hōjō* to a different *shoin* building called the Shūun-ken. On the other side of the corridor, there is an open rectangular courtyard garden laid with fine white gravel raked in straight lines. It features a red, single-flowered camellia and three simple groups of stones. This serves as the front (south) garden of the Shūun-ken, and is known as the Chūkai (Middle Ocean), the given explanation being that the river of life flows here into calmer waters, which nevertheless conceal treacherous rocks – temptations and illusions – on which the unwary might still flounder. This is an island-flecked inland sea, like the one sandwiched between two chief islands of Japan, Honshū and Shikoku.

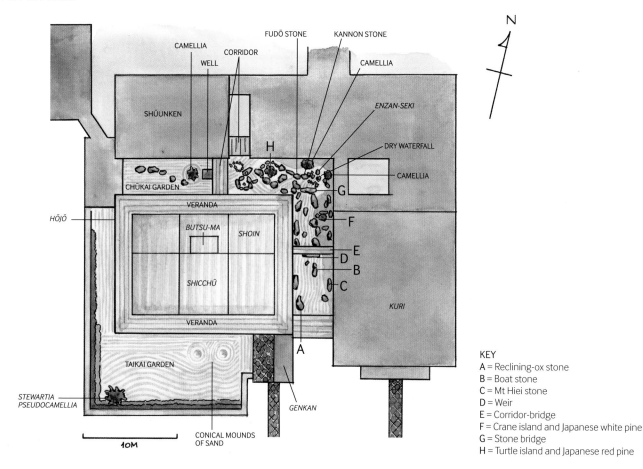

CAMELLIA
WELL
CORRIDOR
FUDŌ STONE
KANNON STONE
CAMELLIA
SHŪUNKEN
ENZAN-SEKI
H
DRY WATERFALL
CHŪKAI GARDEN
CAMELLIA
VERANDA
G
HŌJŌ
BUTSU-MA   SHOIN
F
SHICCHŪ
E
D   B
C
KURI
VERANDA
A
TAIKAI GARDEN
STEWARTIA
PSEUDOCAMELLIA
GENKAN
CONICAL MOUNDS
OF SAND
10M

N

KEY
A = Reclining-ox stone
B = Boat stone
C = Mt Hiei stone
D = Weir
E = Corridor-bridge
F = Crane island and Japanese white pine
G = Stone bridge
H = Turtle island and Japanese red pine

LEFT **Current layout** of the gardens surrounding the *hōjō* at Daisen-in.

RIGHT **This naturally formed** stone basin has acquired the name Butsuban-seki (Buddha's Washbasin Stone). Gautama Buddha is sometimes portrayed in Buddhist art as a newly born infant standing in a basin.

FAR RIGHT **The famous tea master** Sen no Rikyū's design for setting out a stone basin in his tea gardens is said to have been inspired by this cluster of stones, situated next to the Butsuban-seki, on the north side of Daisen-in's *hōjō* (abbot's hall).

The gravel river then turns the corner, follows along the west end of the *hōjō* (abbot's hall) and joins the rectangular garden, which faces the entire length of the south side of the building. This south garden constitutes the formal space that Daisen-in's temple shrine looks out on to. It is enclosed by a double row of pruned hedges and a row of tall trees. These shut out the outside world. The pattern in the white gravel alternates between straight lines and wide undulating curves. This garden is the Taikai (Great Ocean), representing the tranquil open sea. It symbolises the state of nirvana, of enlightenment, where *mu* (emptiness) contains all life in eternity. Two conical mounds of white gravel – a symbol of purity – are located in front of the *shicchū* (central room).

The only other feature of the garden is a pair of *Stewartia pseudocamellia* planted together in the far right-hand corner. This tree is known in Japanese as *natsu-tsubaki* (summer camellia) and also as *shara-no-ki* or *sarasōju*. It is planted in temple gardens as a substitute for the sal tree (*Shorea robusta*), under the flowering branches of which Siddhartha Gautama is said to have died.

The second branch of the symbolic 'river' that flows from the dry waterfall in the north-east section of the garden proceeds along the east side of the *hōjō*. It passes in front of a cluster of stones representing a crane, then under a walled corridor-bridge with a window. The gravel continues under this bridge, where there is a long narrow stone representing a weir. Here the ground level drops slightly. The following section of the garden features a remarkable, boat-shaped stone, behind which there is a triangular stone representing Mt Hiei, the sacred mountain situated to the east of the city of Kyōto.

The Daisen-in garden is conceived on a majestic scale. The Kannon and Fudō stones, the waterfall and the crane stones can all be seen from the *shoin* (study), when its *shōji* (sliding papered door panels) are opened. But it is when the other external wall panels along both the north and east sides of the *hōjō* are removed, along with the *fusuma* (sliding partition walls), which separate the rooms, that a breathtaking panorama is revealed. Only on very special occasions would this have been done. The eye moves along the two branches of the river of life, taking in how the landscape changes and broadens out. It is like viewing a

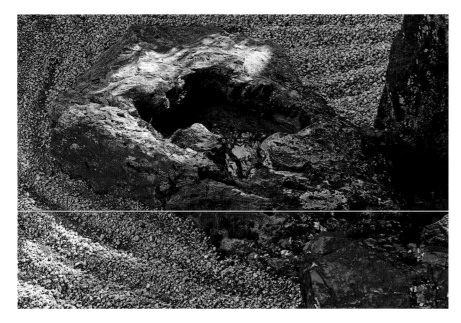

long scroll painting and watching the scene gradually change before one's eyes as the scroll is unrolled.

The oldest part of the garden – the north-east corner – has traditionally been attributed to Kogaku Sōkō, who founded Daisen-in in 1509, the same year he became the seventy-sixth abbot of Daitoku-ji. This monk, a very learned and pious man who had many devoted followers, apparently had a passion for gardens. Temple records mention him collecting rare trees and unusually shaped stones for a garden, although, unfortunately, they are not specific about which garden this may have been. Kogaku Sōkō is known to have begun building a *hōjō* for Daisen-in in 1513, and by 1530 a garden definitely existed, probably on the north side of this building. The question is whether that *hōjō* is the same as the current one. Recent research suggests that the original *hōjō* may very well have stood elsewhere and that it was later moved – perhaps before Kogaku Sōkō's death in 1548, perhaps after – to its present location; it may possibly have been substantially rebuilt.

It is not at all clear whether the founding abbot's garden was included in the move. Many of the stones in the north-east section of the garden are *aoishi*, as chlorite schist is popularly known in Japan. This green-tinged stone, which often has many beautiful markings owing to the presence of bands and folds in the rock, has always been a prized, highly sought-after garden material. It is not local to Kyōto and, therefore, had to be transported to the city at great cost. The sheer number of exquisitely marked, finely shaped and beautifully coloured stones in the garden at Daisen-in constitutes something of an embarrassment of riches, and imparts a feel of ornate splendour to the

garden. There have been suggestions that the garden was moved here *en masse* from elsewhere.

According to an account of Kyōto and its environs published towards the end of the seventeenth century, the Daisen-in garden was originally created for the residence of the Mitsubuchi clan by the celebrated artist Sōami, the shogun Ashikaga Yoshimasa's art expert. The Mitsubuchi family were vassals of the Ashikaga. In 1586, a Mitsubuchi family member became the abbot of Daitoku-ji, and it is conceivable that the stones from their garden were brought at that time to Daisen-in, where it was the custom for the abbots of Daitoku-ji to live. Curiously, the turtle and the crane arrangements are of a different material, possibly local mountain granite, which has led some historians to suggest these stones could have come from Kogaku Sōkō's original garden. But such auspicious images of longevity as the turtle and the crane were very much part of gardens belonging to the nobility, and they could very well have come from the Mitsubuchi garden along with the other stones.

In any case, if it is correct that these stone arrangements did come from the Mitsubuchi garden, it means that the influence of Chinese ink-brush painting styles was already being felt in domestic gardens and that there was a fair amount of crossover between temple gardens and private ones.

It is not possible to know whether the religiously named stones, such as the Kannon stone, might have borne those designations when they were still in the Mitsubuchi garden. Buddhist readings were, perhaps, given to them after their move to Daisen-in, and once the other two gardens – the Chūkai and the Taikai – were added to create a single religious allegory.

THE SOUTH *HŌJŌ* GARDEN

The south *hōjō* (abbot's hall) garden originally served a ceremonial purpose, in much the same way as the open space located in front of the *shinden* (main hall) of tenth- and eleventh-century aristocratic palaces functioned. The south *hōjō* garden was spread with fine Shirakawa gravel, which symbolised purity, and it was kept free of ornament, decoration and plant life. While the open ground in front of a *shinden* was used in welcoming important guests to the palace, the south *hōjō* garden at a Zen Buddhist temple played a central role in the installation ceremony of a new abbot. The new incumbent would enter by the formal gateway, walk across the immaculate white courtyard, step up on to the veranda and enter the *hōjō*, thereby taking possession of it.

By the beginning of the seventeenth century, however, the south garden no longer served this ceremonial purpose, and it came to be considered increasingly as something to be viewed from the *hōjō*. The south garden of the *dai-hōjō* (large hall) at Daitoku-ji is a fine example of this new type of garden. Daitoku-ji burnt down completely in the Ōnin War. Its reconstruction was overseen by the celebrated Zen Buddhist monk Ikkyū Sōjun, who was appointed its abbot in 1474. With the financial backing of Owa Sōrin, a wealthy merchant of the important port city of Sakai on Ōsaka Bay, Ikkyū was able to construct a new *hōjō* to replace the one that had been destroyed. But in 1636 this building was moved, and a new imposing *hōjō* (the *dai-hōjō*) was built to commemorate the approaching third centenary of the death of Daitoku-ji's founding priest, Shūhō Myōchō. The *dai-hōjō*'s south garden, along with its east garden, is thought to have been created shortly after the completion of this new building.

It would be fascinating to know whether Ikkyū's *hōjō* had a south garden and, if so, whether it was in the earlier unadorned style. Sadly, no information has survived. But the south garden of the *dai-hōjō* of 1636 does offer a fascinating glimpse of a transitional phase, when the south garden had become mainly ornamental but nonetheless retained features that served as

reminders of its traditional function. For example, there is a grand, elaborately decorated gateway situated in the south garden wall, so that it faces the *shicchū* (central room) of the building. An invisible path extends from this gate through the garden up to the *dai-hōjō*. No stones or plants stand in the way of this unmarked path. A pair of conical gravel mounds flanks it near the step leading up on to the veranda and into the *shicchū*.

For all intent and purposes, the *dai-hōjō* is actually approached from its west side. This end of the garden is closed off by a wall, and a roofed porch connects the *genkan* (formal entrance) with the veranda of the *dai-hōjō*. This side of the *dai-hōjō*, moreover, is connected to the *kuri* (domestic quarters), which now houses the temple's administrative offices. When standing at the west end of the *dai-hōjō*'s long veranda, the viewer has a long sweeping diagonal view of the south garden, from the broad oval island of moss with two stones immediately in the foreground, across a broad empty expanse of white gravel, over to the simple, two-stone, dry-waterfall arrangement set among tall pruned camellias in the garden's far south-east corner.

At first sight, it seems a rather understated garden. The waterfall does not give a great impression of height, possibly because the waterfall stones have not been placed on raised ground – as in the garden at Daisen-in, for example. The south garden of the *dai-hōjō* at Daitoku-ji is completely flat, thus preserving the original characteristic of the gravelled ceremonial space. But it makes use of this very flatness in order to confuse the viewer's sense of distance. The white gravel symbolises the open sea and the stillness of eternity itself. The waterfall has no water and therefore never runs dry, forever feeding into the symbolic sea. Thus, perpetual motion exists alongside eternal stillness. Time never stops. All things rush towards change and are swallowed up in the great melting pot of the universe, which is symbolised by the calm still sea. Our lives are like the islands of moss floating on the surface of this sea.

Two islands float amid a vast ocean symbolised by the white Shirakawa gravel in the south garden of Daitoku-ji's *dai-hōjō*. The dry waterfall is intended to look remote in the distance. The two gravel cones mark the ceremonial entrance to the *shicchū*, the central room of the *hōjō*.

The strata visible in these stones impart a feeling of dynamic movement to this exquisite stone grouping in the east garden of Daitoku-ji's *dai-hōjō*. There are five stones in this group – an auspicious number.

Two ancient camellias loom up behind the two waterfall stones. They are beautifully pruned and represent the mountainside down which the waterfall tumbles. Originally, it was possible to get a glimpse of the faraway peaks of a mountain range rising in the distance behind the camellias. Indeed, a sweeping panorama of the east half of the city was once visible beyond the double hedge bordering the garden that extends along the entire east length of the *dai-hōjō* (large hall). The viewer could see the pine trees that once lined the banks of the Kamo river and, soaring up in the distance, a hazy blue chain of mountains, with Mt Hiei rising above them all, guarding the city with its sacred presence. The shapes of the distant mountains were mirrored in

The two standing monoliths in the south garden of Daitoku-ji's *dai-hōjō* represent a curtain of falling water. The ancient pruned camellias overshadowing them, together with the other stones and pruned shrubs, help to create the feeling of a mountainous terrain.

大德寺
方丈

the groupings of garden stones, arranged in the sparkling white gravel along the foot of the evergreen hedge. But the double hedge has been allowed to increase in height, and a row of evergreen oaks has grown thick and tall behind it, shutting out the discordant bustle of modern life. It is now a self-contained garden effectively cut off from the world outside the temple.

Two names have traditionally been associated with the south and east gardens of the *dai-hōjō* (large hall) at Daitoku-ji: one being the garden-loving monk Tenyū Shōkō, who was the abbot of Daitoku-ji at the time the new *dai-hōjō* was built; the other being the high-ranking *bushi* (member of the military class), tea master and garden architect Kobori Masakazu, popularly known as Kobori Enshū, who designed the south garden of the *dai-hōjō* at Nanzen-ji. At Nanzen-ji, Enshū demonstrated a deft hand at manipulating the viewer's sense of distance and space, and there is a striking aspect of the east garden of Daitoku-ji's *dai-hōjō* that suggests that the use of forced perspective has been applied here as well. This east garden, which is 21 m/70 ft in length, narrows substantially from north to south, so that when it is viewed from the northernmost corner of the veranda its length is exaggerated. But there is no surviving evidence to show whether Enshū created the east garden or had a hand in designing the south garden. However, he did have a link with Daitoku-ji, for he founded a hermitage on the grounds of one of its sub-temples in 1612.

OPPOSITE A view from the *hōjō* (abbot's hall) of the mountain range that borders the city of Kyōto to the east is shown in this illustration of the south garden of Daitoku-ji's *hōjō* in the 1799 guidebook *Miyako Rinsen Meishō Zue*.

BELOW Leaf-shaped flat stones suggest the stately movement of a vast ocean current. On the right, the ornate gateway originally built for the warlord Toyotomi Hideyoshi's Kyōto palace, the Jukakudai, formerly stood in another part of Daitoku-ji. It was brought here after the original gateway (seen in the 1799 illustration, opposite) was moved in 1868 or 1877 to Konchi-in, where it can still be seen.

As a result of the fire of 1797, the garden walls surrounding the famous south garden of Ryōan-ji's *hōjō* are now ochre-coloured and streaked, as though an enormous, ink-laden *hake* brush has been swept along them. Vertical cracks have also appeared, and in places the surface has flaked off, giving the scorch marks a patterned quality.

RYŌAN-JI

The famous *kare-sansui* (dry-landscape) garden at Ryōan-ji is located on the south side of its *hōjō* (abbot's hall), and it also retains vestiges of the old-style ceremonial south garden. It is totally flat, covered in fine raked Shirakawa gravel, and contains no trees or shrubs. Its fifteen stones are one of the greatest mysteries of Japanese garden history. When did they first make their appearance? Were all fifteen here from the beginning, or did they increase in number over the centuries? Was the garden ever lengthened, widened or otherwise restructured? Were the stones ever rearranged? Suggestions for when the stone garden was first created vary from the middle of the fifteenth century, when the temple was founded, all the way down to the beginning of the seventeenth century. If the Ryōan-ji stone garden could be dated with any accuracy, it would give garden historians a better idea as to when the change in the use of the south *hōjō* garden occurred. Surprisingly — and frustratingly — very little has survived on paper about this remarkable garden.

The temple was founded by the nobleman Hosokawa Katsumoto, who was a high-ranking minister to the shogun Ashikaga Yoshimasa. Ryōan-ji was constructed on the site of a former Buddhist temple, which itself had stood in the grounds of a twelfth-century aristocrat's villa. It was the bitter rivalry between Hosokawa Katsumoto and another powerful warlord that ignited the Ōnin War in 1467, and Ryōan-ji burnt down soon after the conflict began. It was then re-established, and in 1488, fifteen years after Katsumoto's death, his son Hosokawa Masamoto set out to restore the temple's prestige, by appointing a new abbot and initiating a programme of rebuilding. A new *hōjō* was completed in 1499.

The most commonly accepted theory is that the *kare-sansui* garden was created soon after the new *hōjō* was finished. The possibility that some part of a previous garden survived the conflagration of 1467 cannot entirely be ruled out. On the other hand, the warlord Toyotomi Hideyoshi held a flower-viewing

Forced perspective has been employed in the design of Ryōan-ji's stone garden. The ground is tilted so that the walls gradually decrease in height as they converge in the garden's south-west corner. This helps to exaggerate the feeling of depth and distance.

party at the temple in 1588, at which the guests were invited to compose poems about the weeping cherry tree, which was then in full bloom, but no references were made on that occasion to any stone garden. Some garden historians have taken this as an indication that the *kare-sansui* (dry-landscape) garden did not yet exist. The tree was presumably the cherry tree of which the stump can still be found in the moss-covered, rectangular space on the west side of the *hōjō* (abbot's hall). It is recorded, however, that, in that same year, Hideyoshi issued an order that no trees or rocks should be removed from the grounds of Ryōan-ji. There is no way of determining whether the stones mentioned in the order refer to the ones currently in the *kare-sansui* garden, or to some other stones, which may or may not still be somewhere else in the quite extensive grounds of Ryōan-ji. The first written reference to a *kare-sansui* garden at Ryōan-ji appears in a book published in 1681, but it mentions only nine stones, not the full fifteen.

This is not the end of the mystery. There is an illustration of the Ryōan-ji *hōjō* in a guidebook to Kyōto published in 1780, but it depicts a garden on either side of a roofed corridor that leads from a gate in the south garden wall to the *hōjō*. The picture, unfortunately, omits the stones. In February 1797, the *hōjō*, along with the roofed corridor and the gateway, burnt down in a fire that started in the temple's dining hall. The *hōjō* of one of Ryōan-ji's sub-temples was subsequently brought over and reassembled on the site of the lost building. There is a theory that debris from the fire was used as landfill, on top of which the garden stones were relaid , either according to the previous plan or adjusted to suit the new *hōjō*, which appears to have been slightly smaller than the building it replaced. One reason for the landfill theory is that the roof surmounting the south and west garden walls is broader and its eaves deeper than the current height of the walls warrants.

Many accidents of history have contributed to the present appearance of the *kare-sansui* garden at Ryōan-ji. But the layout of the stones appears to be anything but arbitrary. On the contrary, it has been carefully thought out and very skilfully executed. The design becomes apparent when the visitor sits at the eastmost end of the veranda. It is not possible to see all fifteen stones from this spot, but the largest is nearby, while the smaller flatter stones are positioned farther away. The reason for this is to play with the viewer's sense of scale and distance – the garden being designed to create the illusion that it is deeper than it actually is. To this end, the whole garden is slightly tilted: although the gradient is hardly perceptible, the garden slopes downwards from the south wall in the direction of the *hōjō*, and also from the west wall towards the east border of the garden. This results in the two garden walls decreasing ever so slightly in height as they approach the corner where they meet, that is to say, the south-west corner of the garden.

The effect is to make the stones that are the farthest away seem even smaller and more distant. It is as though the groups of stones in the garden are islands dotting an otherwise empty sea. Or perhaps they are the peaks of colossal mountains poking out above the clouds. The fashion for *bonseki*, the

art of creating miniature landscapes in a container, led perhaps to a taste for the kind of smaller understated stones seen in the Ryōan-ji garden. The use of open space in the garden has quite possibly been influenced by a Chinese style of ink-brush painting known as *zanzan jōsui* in Japanese (*cán shān shèng shuī* in Chinese), in which a landscape was not depicted in its entirety but suggested by only a few of its most salient features – the rest of the page being left blank. This style of painting was developed by artists of the Southern Song dynasty such as Baen (Mǎ Yuǎn in Chinese) and Kakei (Xia Gui), and it was extremely influential in Japan.

The attempts made to interpret – to 'understand' – the Ryōan-ji garden have been myriad. There have been theories about the possibility of some numerical symbolism lurking in the grouping of the stones. Religious interpretations have not been lacking. One is that the stones represent sensory phenomena, while the empty space stands for *mu* (emptiness) – the religio-philosophical Buddhist belief that nothing exists as the senses perceive or the mind conceives them. This, it must be noted, is not the same thing as saying nothing exists.

Another theory is that the stones are a reminder of those mental hazards – passions, desires, delusions – that threaten to shipwreck one's efforts to attain enlightenment. Yet another is that the garden is not symbolic of anything, but that the sheer abstractness of its design inspires a meditative state of mind.

It is almost as though visitors to the temple have needed to be reassured that the garden is indeed a work of genius rather than a case of humbug. But this garden encourages the visitor to lay aside value judgments and to look and listen instead. Jewel-like dragonflies hover over the gravel, delicately touching down on the edge of one or another of the silent stones. The dragonflies come for the pond beyond the garden wall, but their presence is, nonetheless, startling and unexpected against the brilliant white background of this dry garden. As the sun trundles across the sky, the ink-black shadows of tree branches spread across the weather-beaten surfaces of the walls and the empty white expanse of gravel. The shadow of a bird flies across the open space, accompanied by a raucous crowing high overhead. There is neither good nor bad. There is only the present moment.

The south garden of Konchi-in's *hōjō* (abbot's hall) was designed to be viewed from the chief reception room. When all the sliding doors are removed, the transom and the floor frame the garden so that it resembles a long scroll painting. In the centre, there is a miniature landscape, representing islands rising out of the sea. This is flanked by a turtle island on the left and a crane island (of which the stone representing the crane's neck is visible) on the right.

KOBORI ENSHŪ AND KONCHI-IN

The Ōnin War, which caused so much damage to the city of Kyōto, was a prelude to a century of political turmoil. The Ashikaga dynasty clung on as nominal governors of Japan until the 1580s, but, in actuality, the country was carved up into numerous small territories, which were ruled by *daimyō* (local feudal lords), who were constantly at war with each other. In 1573, the *daimyō* Oda Nobunaga drove the last Ashikaga shogun out of Kyōto. In 1590, one of Nobunaga's chief generals, Toyotomi Hideyoshi, finally succeeded in crushing the power of the regional *daimyō* and unifying the country under his rule. Hideyoshi had made Ōsaka his stronghold and under his influence, aided by the great wealth of the merchant community in the nearby port of Sakai, there was a great blossoming of the arts in the Ōsaka and Kyōto area. The opulence and verve of the late sixteenth-century artistic style is reflected in the turtle-and-crane garden at Entoku-in, a sub-temple of the Zen Buddhist temple Kōdai-ji, located in the east part of Kyōto close to the Gion quarter. The garden stones, which are of magnificent size, are said to have been brought here from Hideyoshi's Fushimi Castle, which stood to the south of the city of Kyōto. Hideyoshi's passion for the tea ceremony, which was shared by many of his generals, advisers and retainers, also had a great influence on the development of painting, ceramics and architecture, as well as garden design.

Toyotomi Hideyoshi died in 1598, leaving his young son as his heir. This gave his former rival Tokugawa Ieyasu the opportunity to launch his bid for political supremacy. Many of Hideyoshi's former supporters threw their weight behind Ieyasu, who assumed the title of shogun in 1603, and crushed the Toyotomi faction for good in 1615. Ieyasu moved the centre of government to his stronghold Edo (modern-day Tōkyō), and the dynasty he founded ruled Japan until 1867.

The patronage of Tokugawa Ieyasu and his immediate successors, his son Hidetada and grandson Iemitsu, inspired the work of one of Japan's most famous garden designers – Kobori Masakazu, known as Kobori Enshū. Enshū was a *daimyō* (feudal lord), a high-ranking government official and, above all, a celebrated tea master. His father, who came from the area surrounding the north tip of Japan's largest lake, Biwa-ko, had been a retainer of Toyotomi Hideyoshi's brother, but after Hideyoshi's death he shifted his allegiance to Tokugawa Ieyasu. For this, he was rewarded by being made lord of Bichū Matsuyama, the region surrounding what is now the city of Takahashi in the prefecture of Okayama. Enshū succeeded his father in 1604 at the age of twenty-five. In 1619, Enshū gave up Bichū Matsuyama and instead became lord of Ōmi Komuro, near where his family had come from. In 1623, he was made magistrate for Fushimi, south of the city of Kyōto.

As a government official under the shogunate, Enshū was entrusted with major construction projects. He was given responsibility for the upkeep of Tokugawa Ieyasu's personal residence, Sumpu Castle. He worked on the construction of a magnificent new castle in the city of Nagoya, and the creation of a new palace and a garden for Edo Castle. That garden survives as the Ninomaru Garden of the Higashi Gyoen within the Imperial Palace at Tōkyō. In 1624, Enshū was put in charge of the prestigious project of constructing a new palace and remodelling the garden at Nijō Castle in Kyōto, in preparation for a visit from the emperor Go-Mizuno'o, which took place in 1626. He later built a graceful palace garden for Go-Mizuno'o's private residence within the precincts of the Imperial Palace. This garden too survives, although Go-Mizuno'o's buildings have not.

Enshū's connections with the shogunate were not restricted to his rank as *daimyō* and his official duties as building commissioner. As an eminent practitioner of the tea ceremony, he served as tea master to the second Tokugawa shogun Hidetada and to the third, Iemitsu. He also hosted frequent tea ceremonies (especially after he settled in Fushimi as its magistrate), which brought together members of different social groups and ranks, especially aristocrats and high-ranking *bushi* (members of the military class), at a time when the imperial court and the shogunate were still very suspicious of each other. Enshū's distinctive style of tea has been faithfully passed down and is still practised today.

As early as 1618, Enshū was already in correspondence with Ishin Sūden, the abbot of Nanzen-ji in Kyōto. Ishin was a great connoisseur of the tea ceremony. He was also a member of the inner circle of the shogunate. He had been one of Tokugawa Ieyasu's most trusted advisers, and such was his power that he was widely known as the Chancellor in Black – black being the colour of the Buddhist monks' robes in Japan. Nanzen-ji had remained in a poor state of repair since the Ōnin War. Ishin became its abbot in 1605, and with his growing political clout he was able to begin restoring the temple properly. When, in 1611, the Tokugawa shogunate decided that the Imperial Palace in Kyōto should be rebuilt, Nanzen-ji was accorded the honour of being given one of the chief buildings of the old palace to serve as its new *hōjō* (abbot's hall). A hall that had originally belonged to Toyotomi Hideyoshi's Jurakudai Palace in Kyōto, and had subsequently been relocated to Fushimi Castle, was given to Ishin by the shogun Tokugawa Hidetada in the same year. This became the new *hōjō* of Konchi-in, one of Nanzen-ji's sub-temples and Ishin's own private residence.

When Konchi-in was founded in the fifteenth century, it had originally been in a different part of the city, but Ishin had it moved to Nanzen-ji soon after he became its abbot. In 1626, Ishin decided to refurbish the sub-temple in celebration of his having been given an honorary title. A new *hōjō* was built, and in 1629 Enshū created a tea room – the famous Hassō-seki – for a *shoin* (reception hall), which adjoins it. In the same year, Ishin began discussing with Enshū the idea of a south garden for Konchi-in's brand-new *hōjō*.

That garden is Enshū's and Ishin's homage to the Tokugawa dynasty. Set against a wooded incline thickly planted with tall evergreens, it is in the *kare-sansui* (dry-landscape) style, with an extensive stone garden and a wide

The reception rooms of Konchi-in's *hōjō* were designed to accommodate a visit from the shogun and are sumptuously decorated with *fusuma* (sliding partition-wall) paintings by the brothers Kanō Tanyū and Kanō Naonobu. The building is traditionally said to have been a part of Fushimi Castle, but an alternative theory is that it was built during the 1626 refurbishment of Konchi-in.

expanse of raked white gravel in the foreground. Two immense stone groupings occupy most of the stone garden: the one, on the right, symbolises the auspicious crane and is surmounted by a Japanese red pine (*Pinus densiflora*) – a symbol of longevity – while the other, on the left, represents the turtle and is planted with an incredibly gnarled, ancient-looking Chinese juniper (*Juniperus chinensis*) – an emblem of endurance in the pursuit of spiritual enlightenment. The turtle has a head-shaped stone and the juniper tree, which the turtle carries on its back, is believed to be the original, which had been planted on this spot so many centuries ago. The crane has an enormous rectangular stone, which represents its outstretched neck, while other stones suggest the bird's powerful wings lifted in flight. The crane faces eastwards, as though it were flying off in the direction of Edo, the capital of the Tokugawa shogunate.

The two creatures face each other across a large flat rectangular stone of a purplish hue, which serves as a *reihai-seki* (worship stone). This *reihai-seki* is set in front of a miniature landscape representing islands rising out of the sea. There is a *sanzon-seki* (three sacred stones) grouping, with the stones arranged so that they look like a series of mountain peaks. Their juxtaposition with the images of the turtle and crane suggests that they stand for the Islands of the Immortals. At the same time, the presence of the *reihai-seki* implies that the stones in the *sanzon-seki* are meant to represent Buddha and his attendants. But the *reihai-seki* has another purpose. It pays homage to a large shrine, which stands beyond the trees in the background.

ABOVE The crane island at Konchi-in is characterised by a horizontal stone representing a crane's neck outstretched in flight. A triangular stone suggesting its upraised wing is visible under the auspicious Japanese red pine tree (*Pinus densiflora*).

OPPOSITE The turtle and crane islands lie on either side of a delicate miniature seascape, complete with stones representing the steep peaks of the Islands of the Immortals.

This shrine, which was designed by Enshū, is dedicated to the deified spirit of Tokugawa Ieyasu.

The enormous turtle and crane arrangements in the foreground nearly dwarf the central stone landscape, over which they appear to stand sentinel. The extreme contrast is, however, intentional and was meant to give depth to the overall composition. The garden was designed to be viewed primarily from the inner chamber of a resplendent set of reception rooms located on the west side of the building. When the *fusuma* (sliding partition walls) are removed, along with all the external *shōji* (sliding papered doors), the entire length of the garden is visible from the raised dais in the inner reception chamber. The area of white gravel becomes invisible behind the projecting veranda, and the turtle and crane arrangements, along with the stone landscape in between them, assume the appearance of one long narrow scroll painting in vivid colour.

The Konchi-in garden was completed in 1632. Ishin's journal noted gifts of prized pieces of stone donated to Konchi-in by various *daimyō* (feudal lord) around the country. This gives an indication of how important Ishin was seen

to be by those men whose position now depended on remaining on good terms with the Tokugawa shogunate.

Enshū was project manager for the Konchi-in south garden, while day-to-day supervision of the work was put in the hands of one of Enshū's retainers, an experienced man by the name of Murase Sasuke. Another expert involved in the construction of the Konchi-in garden was the master stoneworker known as Kentei. In all likelihood, it was he who made the actual decisions about where to put each stone, based on Enshū's overall concept. Kentei was a *senzui-kawaramono* who received the name he is remembered by ('Kentei' can be literally translated as 'Wise Garden') from the emperor Go-Yōzei in recognition of his work on the Sanbō-in garden at the Kyōto temple Daigo-ji. (Daigo-ji was not a Zen temple but belonged to the Shingon school of Buddhism.) The Sanbō-in garden is a pond garden and it was designed, moreover, by the warlord Toyotomi Hideyoshi. Garden styles were widely shared by temples of different schools, as well as between temples and private residences, and men such as Kentei were employed wherever their expertise was required.

Enshū worked with another garden expert, Gyokuen, who was a Buddhist monk of the Nichiren school. Despite belonging to a non-Zen sect, Gyokuen is believed to have designed the south garden of the *hōjō* at Zakke-in, a sub-temple belonging to the Zen Buddhist temple Myōshin-ji in Kyōto. This garden is a stone garden in the Ryōan-ji style, only its austerity is softened by the inclusion of azaleas among the stones. Although it is now covered in moss, it is quite possible that it was originally gravelled over, as is the flat courtyard *kare-sansui* (dry-landscape) garden that Gyokuen created at Myōren-ji, his own Nichiren Buddhist temple. There, Gyokuen used sixteen stones of a rugged dark complexion, set in seven groups amid white Shirakawa gravel. The effect is solemn and grave and yet very beautiful in its sternness. It is usually described as a garden representing the Sixteen *Rakan*, a group of Buddhist holy men venerated particularly in Zen Buddhism, but not exclusively so. The Myōren-ji garden shows how the flat *kare-sansui* style was spreading beyond the confines of Zen temples.

KOBORI ENSHŪ AND KOHŌ-AN

The fact that Kobori Enshū was a renowned tea master was reflected in the design of the gardens and tea rooms he created for Kohō-an, his family temple at Daitoku-ji. Enshū first founded Kohō-an in 1612, in the grounds of Ryōkō-in, a pre-existing sub-temple of Daitoku-ji. He held tea gatherings there, but, being cramped for space, he moved his temple to its present location in 1643. He hoped to retire there, but at the time he was still busily occupied in Edo (modern-day Tōkyō), and the actual building of the temple and its gardens was left to one of his sons. It was not until the spring of 1645, two years before his death, that Enshū was able to return to the Kyōto area.

Kohō-an can be translated as the 'Hermitage of the Solitary Boat with the Reed-Woven Roof'. The name evokes the idea of spiritual tranquillity, but it is, at the same time, a reference to Biwa-ko, the great lake from the north shores of which Enshū's family originated. This lake and the famous scenic views associated with it, provided the inspiration behind the design of many of Kohō-an's rooms and gardens. For example, Enshū did not use white gravel in the otherwise traditional south garden of the *hōjō* (abbot's hall), allowing the bare red soil to represent the waters of the lake. Along the rear of the garden, there are two long straight low hedges of staggered heights. There is another even lower, trimmed hedge just in front of the *hōjō* building. These hedges are intended to suggest the surf rolling in across a foreshore. Originally, it was possible to look out over this garden and see in the distance a mountain called Funaoka-yama (Boat-Hill Mountain), but it is no longer visible because of the tall trees that now surround Kohō-an.

The lake theme is echoed in the name of Kohō-an's splendid principal tea room, the Bōsen, which literally means 'to forget the fish trap'. The name is derived from a saying attributed to the Chinese philosopher Zhuangzi: 'In catching the fish, one forgets the fish trap.' That is, one forgets the means when one is concentrating on the act: in attaining enlightenment, one no longer pays attention to mere words – to the volumes of religious expositions, *kōan* and sermons. It is a reminder to focus on the present moment and on what is happening here and now.

The Bōsen is in the elegant style of a *shoin* (formal study or reception room), while incorporating certain rustic touches that hark back to the simplicity of the style of tea ceremony exemplified by the great sixteenth-century tea master Sen no Rikyū, whom Enshū is supposed to have met as a boy. The room is designed so that sunlight reflects off the surface of the water in the water basin next to the veranda and on to the ceiling, which is made of wood polished, with a mixture of sand and finely pulverised seashells, to a silvery sheen. The Bōsen is meant to have the ambience of a passenger compartment on board a *maruko-bune*, the type of wooden ship that used to ply the waters of Lake Biwa.

The Bōsen is approached from the outside along a row of stepping stones, and the entrance on to the veranda is kept low with the use of *shōji* (screens consisting of translucent paper pasted over a wooden frame), which have been suspended from the ceiling, leaving an opening just high enough for guests to enter on their knees. This opening also acts as a wide but narrow horizontal window, such as one that might have been found on board a *maruko-bune*.

The garden of the Bōsen tea room is designed to be viewed from indoors through this horizontal entrance-cum-window. It is an exquisitely simple garden, with a stone basin and a stone lantern set among lustrous, blackish grey pebbles, which form a vivid contrast to the greenery of the tall trimmed hedge positioned like a standing screen behind the lantern. The dark pebbles can be read as representing the waters of Lake Biwa, and there is, behind the stone lantern, a low Mt Fuji-shaped stone with gently sloping sides. This stone is a reference not to Mt Fuji *per se* but to Mikami-yama, known as the Ōmi-Fuji, or the Mt Fuji of the land of Ōmi, which rises above a flat plain not far from the south-west shores of Lake Biwa.

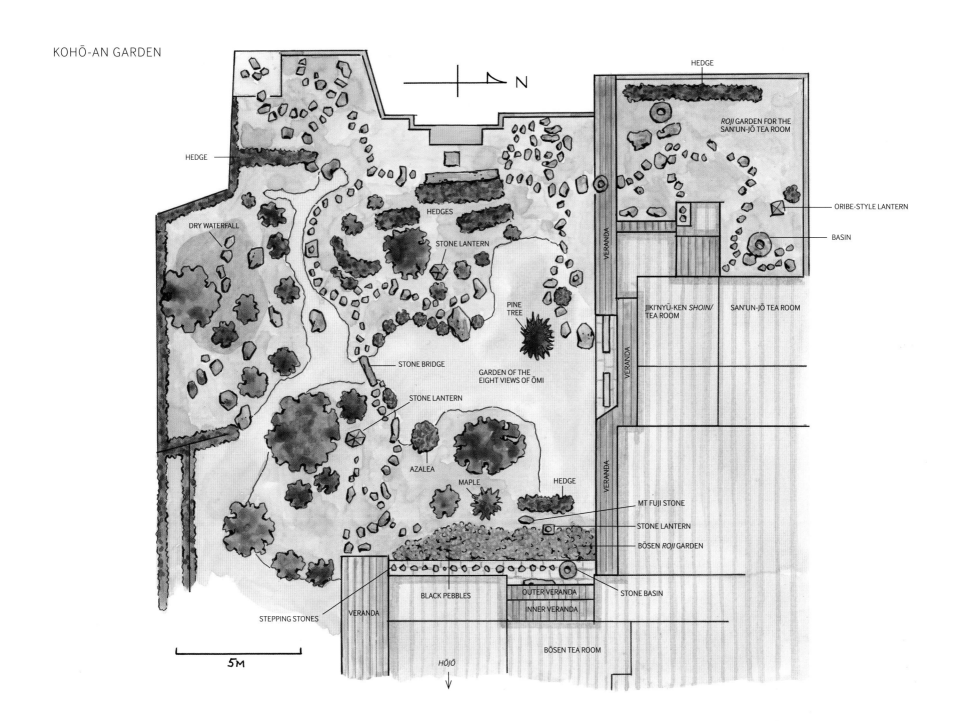

Plan of the Ōmi-hakkei-no-niwa (Garden of the Eight Views of Ōmi) and the tea gardens at Kohō-an, in their current form.

KOHŌ-AN GARDEN

N

HEDGE

ROJI GARDEN FOR THE SAN'UN-JŌ TEA ROOM

HEDGE

DRY WATERFALL

HEDGES

STONE LANTERN

ORIBE-STYLE LANTERN

BASIN

PINE TREE

JIKI'NYŪ-KEN *SHOIN/* TEA ROOM

SAN'UN-JŌ TEA ROOM

VERANDA

STONE BRIDGE

GARDEN OF THE EIGHT VIEWS OF ŌMI

STONE LANTERN

VERANDA

AZALEA

MAPLE

HEDGE

MT FUJI STONE

STONE LANTERN

BŌSEN *ROJI* GARDEN

5M

BLACK PEBBLES

OUTER VERANDA

STONE BASIN

STEPPING STONES

VERANDA

INNER VERANDA

BŌSEN TEA ROOM

HŌJŌ

The small hedge behind the stone lantern screens the rest of the garden from the view of those sitting in the Bōsen tea room. In fact, there is quite an extensive garden, called the Garden of the Eight Views of Ōmi, which is intended to be viewed from a different room, a *shoin* (reception room)-cum-tea room called the Jiki'nyū-ken. This *kare-sansui* (dry-landscape) garden is embellished with beautifully pruned, low pine trees, stones and shrubs, which are designed to remind the beholder of the eight famous scenic views around Lake Biwa; these eight views were established in the seventeenth century under the influence of the famous Chinese set of scenic views, the Eight Views of Xiaoxiang. The Garden of the Eight Views of Ōmi is a *kare-sansui* garden, but it is not laid with gravel in the usual way — the red soil of the garden being allowed to represent the waters of the lake in its tranquil moments. A path of stepping stones leads from the Jiki'nyū-ken around this garden, along the 'shore' of the 'lake', as it were, and over a low stone bridge, finally linking up with the stepping stones leading to the Bōsen tea room. In this regard, the Garden of the Eight Views acts as the Bōsen's outer tea garden, while the garden immediately in front of the tea room serves as the inner tea garden.

BELOW The Kōrin-an is Jikō-in's principal tea room, and it adjoins the north-east corner of the temple's *shoin* (reception hall) building. This shows the area where the host would sit to prepare the tea. A square portion of the tatami matting conceals the hearth on which a kettle would have been placed to boil water.

OPPOSITE This view of Jikō-in's thatched, two-storey gateway is from the *shoin* building. The gateway was brought here from a castle that formerly belonged to the uncle of the founder of Jikō-in, Katagiri Sekishū.

THE TEA GARDEN AT JIKŌ-IN

One of the loveliest temple gardens in Japan is found at Jikō-in, in the town of Yamato-kōriyama in Nara prefecture. This temple, which was built between 1663 and 1671, is a wonderful testament to the artistic vision of its founder, Katagiri Sadamasa (known as Sekishū). Jikō-in is a Zen Buddhist temple belonging to the Daitoku-ji branch of the Rinzai school, but the temple does not have a *hōjō* (abbot's hall). Instead, it is the *shoin* (reception hall) building that is the centre of this temple. The principal room of the *shoin* and the garden on to which it faces constitute the reception area for the tea room, which is attached to the north-east corner of the same building. The temple's shrine, dedicated to the Gautama Buddha, is found in a separate building, the *hon-dō* (sanctuary), which lies on the north side of the *shoin* building, and is separated from it by a courtyard garden.

Like Kobori Enshū, Sekishū was a *daimyō* (feudal lord). He, too, spent some time as a government official under the shogunate, overseeing the rebuilding of the temple Chion-in in Kyōto. He was, moreover, a distinguished tea master, and later in life he was appointed tea instructor to the fourth shogun of the Tokugawa dynasty, Ietsuna. Sekishū had become critical of over-refinement of taste, which had been spreading among his fellow *daimyō* tea masters under the influence of the likes of Enshū. He wanted to see a return to Sen no Rikyū's simplicity of style. Yet Sekishū remained extremely conscious of social rank. Rikyū's preference for a rustic style reflected his strong belief that social rank should be kept out of the tea room. For Rikyū, the simplicity of the rustic hermitage was an equaliser: it reduced everyone to their essential humanity and the *busshō* (Buddha nature), which is shared by all beings. For Sekishū, however, too much rusticity verged on squalor. He believed strongly that it was beneath the dignity of people of high rank to assume the trappings of poverty, even as an ascetic stance.

Sekishū built Jikō-in in memory of his father, from whom he inherited his title in 1627. In it, he found his own way of marrying a simple country charm with refined elegance. The atmosphere is very carefully orchestrated from the moment visitors first enter the outer gate. A shady path passes between high earth banks held together by the massive snaky roots of the tall trees, which cast their shade over the paving stones. A corner is turned, and the visitor comes to the double-storey, inner gateway, which was brought there from a castle that had formerly belonged to the family. This gateway has thatched roofs, and when the visitor passes through the gate they see that the lovely *shoin* (reception hall) building too has a thatched roof. But this building is far from being a mere farmhouse. Inside, it is graciously proportioned with large airy rooms: in the way traditional Japanese buildings were constructed, the *shoin* building has *fusuma* (sliding partition walls) so that the rooms can be turned into a single enormous space, which opens – when the outside shutters and the *shōji* (sliding papered door panels) are also removed – on to the garden along its entire south and east sides. The garden is exceedingly simple in style, consisting of immaculately raked white gravel and beautifully trimmed mounds of azaleas and other evergreens.

It is customary in a tea garden to have a *koshi-kake machi-ai* (small roofed bench) somewhere along the path. It provides a spot where guests can join one another before moving on to the tea room. The garden at Jikō-in, however, flouts convention, and dispenses with a bench of this kind. Instead, the *shoin*'s east veranda assumes the role of meeting place for guests.

Although it is possible to stroll around the garden, it is principally designed to be appreciated from the *shoin*. However, there are some unpretentious stepping stones that lead from the east veranda around to the left to a low bamboo gate. This, in fact, is the principal approach to the tea room itself. Through the bamboo gate, there is a tiny forecourt in front of the square entrance to the tea room. This tea room can also be accessed from inside the *shoin* building, but this is not the point.

The purpose of a Japanese tea garden is to give guests the time and opportunity to put the distractions of their daily lives to one side. This is exactly what the *shoin* and garden at Jikō-in do: they encourage the visitor to stop worrying about the past or fretting about the future, and to experience the present moment to the full, to breathe in the fresh greenery and listen to the birdsong in spring and the croaking of the frogs in the early summer. The act of viewing a garden is essentially similar to both the practice of the tea ceremony and of *zazen* (sitting meditation), for all of these activities demand the participant's total concentration. There can be no half measures.

LEFT The tall stone basin by the east veranda of Jikō-in's *shoin* (reception hall) indicates the start of a short path leading through a bamboo gate into the inner tea garden of the Kōrin-an tea room; another beautiful stone basin is located next to stepping stones from the *shoin* into the south garden (below left); a view from Jikō-in's *hon-dō* (sanctuary) across the courtyard garden towards the *shoin* building, with the second of Jikō-in's tea rooms on the right (below right).

OPPOSITE A window frames a view of the landscape towards the east of Jikō-in.

OPPOSITE BELOW The *shoin* building is designed so that *fusuma* (sliding partition walls) and *shōji* (sliding papered door panels) can be removed to reveal a panoramic view of the south garden.

JIKŌ-IN

Jikō-in, located in Nara prefecture, looks out on to a sweeping panoramic view of the Yamato plain, bordered in the far distance by a range of hazy, blue-grey mountains. This plain used to be rich farmland. This is the ancient heartland of Japan and the cradle of its civilisation. The garden celebrates this scenery: the pruned shrubs in the garden mimic the shapes of the far-off mountains, while the white gravel represents the fertile fields of rice. Sadly, the paddy fields have now largely been built over, and traffic clogs the main road that passes right below the temple garden. This is a borrowed landscape that has changed beyond all recognition. But Jikō-in has not shut away the view behind a green hedge, as other temples in a similar predicament have been tempted to do. The temple has not turned its back on the modern world nor – one fervently hopes – on the people who inhabit it.

SOME EXAMPLES OF EARLY NINETEENTH-CENTURY ZEN TEMPLE GARDENS

With the publishing industry taking off in Japan towards the end of the seventeenth century, illustrated garden manuals began to appear, and these helped to disseminate knowledge about traditional gardening styles. Alongside the familiar pond-and-*tsukiyama* (man-made hillocks) varieties of landscape garden, in which ponds had to be dug and hillocks built up, it is interesting that some of the earliest eighteenth-century books already mentioned the concept of the flat garden, in which gravel is employed to symbolise a large body of water (usually the sea), while stones and a selection of plants are used to fashion the landscape. Such flat gardens came to be known as *hira-niwa*, in contrast to the contoured pond-and-*tsukiyama* garden. These books helped to popularise the style of garden exemplified by the south gardens of the *hōjō* (abbot's hall) at Ryōan-ji and Daitoku-ji, for example (as well as the Nichiren Buddhist temple Myōren-ji), taking it out of temples and into domestic contexts.

The categories were far from rigid, of course, and the various styles were adapted for practical use. An example is Tōkai-an, a prestigious sub-temple of Myōshin-ji. Although the sub-temple was founded in 1484, a set of gardens was created for it only in 1814, by a Zen Buddhist monk called Tōboku Sōho. He had picked up his gardening techniques from an expert from Edo, whom he had met at a temple where he was training.

At Tōkai-an, Tōboku created two gardens surrounding the south-west corner of the temple's *shoin* (reception hall). One is a *kare-sansui* (dry-landscape) garden with moss. It features a Buddhist, *sanzon-seki* (three sacred stones) arrangement and also, towards the right-hand side of the garden, three raised mounds, representing the Daoist Islands of the Immortals. It is, therefore, not a *hira-niwa*, strictly speaking, but neither is it a traditional *tsukiyama* hill garden, nor does it have a dug pond.

The other garden is a *hira-niwa*, and a classic of its kind. It is a diminutive courtyard garden with nothing more than raked gravel and seven stones. It is surrounded by verandas and corridors on all four sides, making it possible to walk all the way around it and view it from every angle. The stones are aligned in a row on an east–west axis; but each stone points in a slightly different direction. With the smallest of the stones in the middle of the row, the two groups of three stones at either end seem to pivot around it like the blades of a propeller on a *take-tombo* (bamboo-dragonfly toy) – an effect that is emphasised by the pattern in which the gravel has been raked.

TŌKAI-AN GARDEN

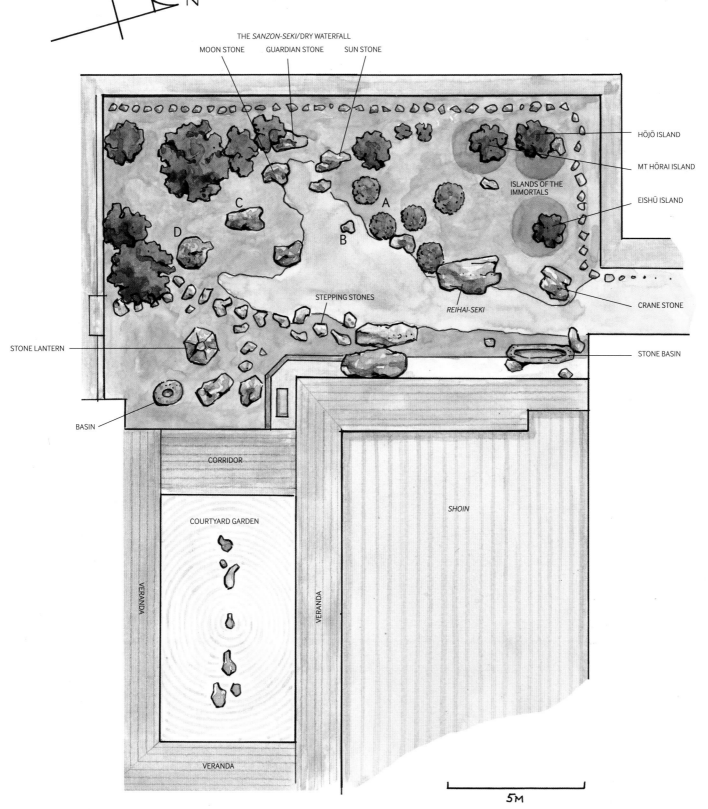

THE *SANZON-SEKI*/DRY WATERFALL

MOON STONE   GUARDIAN STONE   SUN STONE

HŌJŌ ISLAND

MT HŌRAI ISLAND

ISLANDS OF THE IMMORTALS

EISHŪ ISLAND

CRANE STONE

REIHAI-SEKI

STEPPING STONES

STONE BASIN

STONE LANTERN

BASIN

CORRIDOR

COURTYARD GARDEN

VERANDA

VERANDA

SHOIN

VERANDA

5M

THE GARDEN OF THE KAISAN-DŌ AND FUMON-IN, TŌFUKU-JI

At Tōfuku-ji, there is a courtyard garden with the most unusual combination of a flat *kare-sansui* (dry-landscape) garden paired with a miniature pond one. This garden is shared by the Kaisan-dō (the mausoleum of Tōfuku-ji's thirteenth-century founding abbot, Enni Bennen) and a monastic residence called the Fumon-in. A straight path, which leads from a two-storeyed gateway up to the Kaisan-dō, separates the two gardens. On the right-hand side, there is a miniature pond garden, criss-crossed with diminutive stone bridges, and planted with salmon-pink azaleas and purple *Iris laevigata*. The other side of the path is startlingly different: the flat, dry, *kare-sansui* garden is laid with gravel raked geometrically into a traditional Japanese *ichimatsu* (chequerboard) pattern. The austerity of this side of the garden is tempered, however, by a magnificent specimen tree, a *mokkoku* (*Ternstroemia gymnanthera*), around which there are azaleas and an imposing group of stones representing the auspicious crane and turtle.

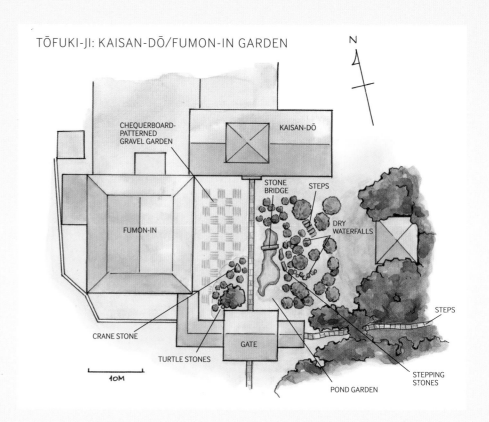

TŌFUKI-JI: KAISAN-DŌ/FUMON-IN GARDEN

N

CHEQUERBOARD-PATTERNED GRAVEL GARDEN

KAISAN-DŌ

STONE BRIDGE

STEPS

DRY WATERFALLS

FUMON-IN

CRANE STONE

TURTLE STONES

GATE

POND GARDEN

STEPS

STEPPING STONES

10M

OPPOSITE Plan of the courtyard garden of the Kaisan-dō and the Fumon-in at Tōfuku-ji in its current form.

RIGHT The crane stone, representing a wing, serves as a focal point for the garden shared by the Kaisan-dō and the Fumon-in at Tōfuku-ji.

FAR RIGHT The miniature pond on the east side of the path leading from the gateway to the Kaisan-dō provides a vivid contrast to the dry gravel garden.

BELOW A view of the garden and the gateway from the north end of Fumon-in's veranda.

THE TWENTIETH CENTURY:
SHIGEMORI MIREI AND NAKANE KINSAKU

The Tokugawa shogunate fell in 1867. In the following year, the emperor Meiji formally assumed power, and a new governmental structure was adopted based on European models. These upheavals impoverished many Buddhist temples, which under the shogunate had had an administrative role within their local communities. The new imperial government wanted to establish Shintoism as the state religion, and it introduced a policy of aggressively curtailing the activities of Buddhist temples. This triggered many savage attacks on temples, often led by members of the public. A great deal of property was destroyed. In 1871, Buddhist temples had all their land, except that on which their temple buildings stood, confiscated by the state. Thus, they were deprived of an important source of income. Prized temple treasures were sold off. Many temples were dissolved, while others became badly neglected or were abandoned altogether.

In the early 1930s, the rundown state of many temple gardens in Kyōto came to the attention of a young aspiring artist by the name of Shigemori Mirei. At the time, he was just beginning to establish a name for himself in Kyōto as a proponent of a new avant-garde style of *ikebana* (traditional Japanese flower arranging). He had a deep love of Japanese painting and the tea ceremony, and took a serious interest in the history of garden design in Japan. In 1932, he co-founded the Kyōto Rinsen Kyōkai, an association promoting research into historic gardens. Then, in late September 1934, the Muroto typhoon struck, bringing widespread devastation to west parts of Japan, especially around the cities of Ōsaka, Kōbe and Kyōto. Shigemori became convinced of the need to survey important old gardens before they were lost forever in another natural disaster. Between 1936 and 1938, he personally catalogued more than 350 gardens, and in 1971, at the age of seventy-five, he undertook a second series of surveys, encompassing nearly 130 more gardens.

Shigemori became a prolific and extremely influential garden architect. Many of the gardens he created during his forty-year career were for private residences, including his own in Kyōto, which is now a museum. He also designed gardens for schools, hotels, *ryokan* (traditional-style Japanese inns), restaurants, meeting halls and, even, the occasional fire station. His finest works include the Hachijin Garden at the historic Kishiwada Castle in 1953. Shigemori also created gardens for several Shinto shrines such as Kasuga Taisha in Nara, in the 1930s, and Matsuo Taisha, in Kyōto, which was the last work he undertook. But Shigemori is best remembered for the gardens he designed for Zen Buddhist temples such as Tōfuku-ji, its sub-temples Ryōgin-an, Reiun-in and Kōmyō-in, and Zuihō-in (a sub-temple of Daitoku-ji). He also participated in the restoration of historically important gardens including Shōden-ji in Kyōto and Ikō-ji in Shimane prefecture in the west of Japan. His 1939 recreation of the south garden of the *hōjō* (abbot's hall) at Funda-in – another Tōfuku-ji sub-temple – has attracted some controversy, not least because the garden was traditionally attributed to the fifteenth-century artist–monk Sesshū.

At the heart of Shigemori's work was his fascination with the traditions of the *kare-sansui* (dry-landscape) style of garden. The south *hōjō* garden at Tōfuku-ji is a superb example of his reinterpretation of the seventeenth-century *hōjō* garden seen, for example, at Daitoku-ji and Nanzen-ji. In 1939, extensive restoration work at Tōfuku-ji was coming to an end, and the abbot called in Shigemori to organise the front (south) *hōjō* garden. The temple had had many fires since its foundation in the mid-thirteenth century and had lost its main buildings once again in a conflagration in 1881. The *hōjō* had been rebuilt in 1890, and in 1909 the formal gateway, which is set in the south *hōjō* garden wall, had been given to the temple by the wife of emperor Meiji. A path of square paving stones led from this gate to the veranda of the *hōjō*. Shigemori had these stones removed and, thereby, he turned the garden, which had had a mainly practical function, into a decorative one viewed principally from the *hōjō*.

Isamu Noguchi, the Japanese-American artist and designer, described the north garden of Tōfuku-ji's *hōjō* (abbot's hall) as being Mondrian-esque in its effect. It was designed by Shigemori Mirei.

RIGHT and BELOW RIGHT Shigemori Mirei
gave the name Hassō-no-niwa (Garden of
the Eight Phases) to the four gardens he
created for Tōfuku-ji's *hōjō* (abbot's hall).
The Eight Phases refer to the eight stages
of Gautama Buddha's life. The south garden
comprises stone groupings representing
four Daoist Islands of the Immortals (right)
and five moss-covered hillocks, symbolising
Kyōto's main Zen Buddhist temples
(below right).

OPPOSITE In the west garden of the *hōjō*
is a chequerboard pattern of Satsuki azaleas
(*Rhododendron indicum*). The bridge,
which can be seen in the background is the
famous Tsūten-kyō; rebuilt in 1961, it spans
a ravine that runs through the middle of the
Tōfuki-ji grounds.

One half of Shigemori's south *hōjō* (abbot's hall) garden is very stark in style, with raked white gravel representing a wild ocean and massive, curiously weathered stones symbolising the Islands of the Immortals. To the traditional three – Hōrai, Hōjō and Eishū – he added a fourth island, Koryō. Jagged and severe, the stones suggest islands relentlessly buffeted by the ocean waves. Over on the right-hand side of the garden, Shigemori created five moss-covered *tsukiyama* (mounds), which he explained were meant to symbolise the *Gozan* (Five Mountains) – the five main Zen Buddhist temples in Kyōto as established by the Ashikaga shogunate in the fourteenth century. Shigemori very cleverly juxtaposed the soft contours of these moss-covered hillocks with the starkness and angularity of the stones at the other end of the garden.

The paving stones that Shigemori had removed from the south garden were taken to the north side of the *hōjō*. Utilising the very awkwardly shaped piece of ground lying between the building and the edge of a precipice, Shigemori created a remarkably original garden, which the Japanese-American artist, sculptor and designer Isamu Noguchi lauded as being very Mondrian in style. Shigemori set the square paving stones in moss in a chequerboard pattern that gradually breaks up, so that towards the right-hand side of the garden it seems that stones are hurtling through empty space. The contrast between the fresh green moss and the white paving stones is strikingly beautiful.

The chequerboard pattern is called the *ichimatsu-moyō* in Japanese, and it is a traditional one. It is repeated in the west garden of the *hōjō* (abbot's

ABOVE These Satsuki azaleas (*Rhododendron indicum*) originally grew in an expanse of white gravel, but moss has since been allowed to colonise the west garden of Tōfuki-ji's *hōjō* (abbot's hall). The design of this garden is the reverse of the north one, in which stone is used for the squares and vegetation for the background.

OPPOSITE The columns in the east garden of the *hōjō* represent the celestial Big Dipper. When designing it, Shigemori Mirei reused the foundation stones of a former temple outhouse, to demonstrate the virtues of frugality and humility. Farther to the right (but out of this picture) is a hedge symbolising the Milky Way.

hall), which Shigemori also covered with white gravel. He then planted azaleas clipped into perfect squares in among the gravel, creating a chequerboard effect in 3D. The fourth garden he made for the *hōjō* can be found on the east side of the corridor that leads from the *kuri* (domestic quarters) to the *hōjō*. There, he arranged seven cylindrical pieces of stone in the pattern of the stars constituting the Big Dipper.

As great as Shigemori Mirei's influence was on the twentieth-century gardening world in Japan, he was not the only garden historian-cum-designer to combine scholarship, erudition, a fine eye for design and down-to-earth practical skills. Nakane Kinsaku is perhaps best known for the expansive landscape garden he created between 1969 and 1972 for the Adachi Museum

of Art in Shimane prefecture. But he is also important for the major role he played in the preservation of many of the outstanding historic gardens in Kyōto, including the pond garden at Kinkaku-ji in 1956 and the Tenryū-ji garden in the following year. These occasions provided an invaluable opportunity for archaeological work to be done on these sites. But his task was not just unravelling the past. The question of restoration invariably involved the problem of which historical period to take the restoration back to. Nakane was instrumental in the decision made in 1978 at Ryōan-ji, for example, when the garden walls were re-roofed with roof shingles instead of burnished clay tiles. As more and more research is done into old gardens, the question of whether to restore or rebuild becomes all the more acute. Some gardens have changed

DAISHIN-IN SUB-TEMPLE, MYŌSHIN-JI

Daishin-in is an ancient *tacchū* (sub-temple) of Myōshin-ji in Kyōto. It was originally founded in the second half of the fifteenth century, but it was brought to Myōshin-ji a century later by the military commander and *daimyō* (feudal lord) Hosokawa Fujitaka (known as Yūsai). For many centuries, Daishin-in provided lodgings for monks coming up to Myōshin-ji from the provinces, as well as to itinerant Buddhist monks. It still carries on the tradition, providing room and board in its *shoin* (reception hall) – the Tanga-ryō.

In 1965, Nakane Kinsaku created an exquisite south garden for this building. It is in the *kare-sansui* (dry-landscape) style, yet Nakane contoured the terrain, creating higher ground in the garden's south-east corner, where there is a *sanzon-seki* (three sacred stones) arrangement and a *reihai-seki* (worship stone) in front of it. The flowing current of a broad river is represented by the white gravel. The riverbank is beautifully curved – the tradition of giving garden ponds a sinuous shoreline goes back to at least the eighth century. This garden is a wonderful example of what can be done in the smallest of spaces.

RIGHT This garden is known as the 'A-un' Garden – *a-un* being the Japanese transliteration of the mystic Buddhist sound *om*. The name implies that the green moss and the white gravel, while remaining distinct, come together to form a single unity, just like the principles of yin and yang.

OPPOSITE The three stones along the back fence make up the *sanzon-seki*. At the foot of the central stone is the flat, oblong *reihai-seki*. At the same time that it stands for Buddha and his attendants, the *sanzon-seki* also represents a waterfall, which flows into the river, symbolised by the white gravel.

BELOW Crepe myrtle (*Lagerstroemia indica*) is a popular garden plant in Japan, where it is known as the *sarusuberi* (monkey slide).

As well as this garden, Daishin-in is famous for its two Kirishima azaleas planted in 1634, at the same time the temple's *hon-dō* (sanctuary) was built. The two trees still turn scarlet with blossoms every year in late April. The old and the new continue to bear witness to the active spiritual life of the temple.

more than others over the centuries. Trees die, moss invades and garden stones become loose in their moorings and collapse. Other stones are missing, because they have been plundered long ago. Where there are old drawings, it is possible to get an idea of how a garden looked in the past. Yet just because a particular picture of a garden has survived is not in itself sufficient justification for a garden to be restored according to it.

Most visitors to Daisen-in – the Daitoku-ji sub-temple with the famous *kare-sansui* (dry-landscape) garden – do not realise just how much the present appearance of the garden owes to artistic decisions made by Nakane Kinsaku. The garden on the east flank of the *hōjō* (abbot's hall) has a corridor-bridge, which divides the north-east part of the garden (featuring a dry waterfall) from the lower section with the boat-shaped stone and a triangular stone representing Mt Hiei. This corridor-bridge is walled, but has one enormous bell-shaped window, which – when the *shōji* (sliding papered panels) are drawn open – allows a glimpse of the dry waterfall from the lower garden. A rare drawing of the Daisen-in garden made sometime during the reign of the Tokugawa shogunate shows this corridor-bridge *in situ*. It would have provided direct access to the *shoin* (abbot's formal study) for private guests. But sometime after 1880, perhaps as late as 1905, the structure was moved to the southernmost end of the east garden. This meant that the garden now formed one continuum from the dry waterfall, past the island representing the crane, to the stone weir and then on to the boat stone and the Mt Hiei stone.

In 1959, the *hōjō* underwent major restoration work, and Nakane was asked to advise on the garden. He decided that the corridor-bridge should be restored to its former location, as indicated in the old drawing. This was carried out between February and April 1961. But some of his fellow garden historians were critical of this decision, arguing that the garden had worked better as one long continuum, without the corridor-bridge acting as a partition that divided it into separate sections. Nakane was dismissive of these objections. But there is a genuine issue here, because not enough information has survived to indicate whether the corridor-bridge was part of the overall design of the *hōjō* garden when the garden stones were first brought there, or whether the structure was itself a later addition, which was then moved at the end of the nineteenth century.

Kōdai-ji in Kyōto has introduced a unique way of bringing the past and the present together. This Zen Buddhist temple was founded in 1606 by the widow of Toyotomi Hideyoshi, and it possesses a dramatic, seventeenth-century pond garden designed around the theme of the crane and the turtle. In 1988, a ten-year project to restore the grounds of the temple was entrusted to the garden architect Kitayama Yasuo. The temple was opened to the public in 1989, after the first year of work.

One of Kitayama's tasks was to deal with the south *hōjō* garden, which had been rebuilt in 1912. This was a rectangular walled garden, but it had become waterlogged and choked with knee-high vegetation. Kitayama improved the drainage and turned it into a white gravelled garden, with a pair of conical gravel mounds, as at Daitoku-ji and Daisen-in. There is now a moss-covered area at the west end of the garden, planted with a weeping cherry tree, and another at the other end with a *kare-sansui*-style arrangement of stones.

Every year, for a month in the springtime and again in autumn, the grounds of Kōdai-ji are lit up in the evenings, and the gravelled south *hōjō* garden becomes the setting for an art installation. An artist or a landscape architect is invited to create an artwork using the gravel garden as a canvas. No restrictions are placed on what its theme should be – it is not required in any way to be Buddhist or religious in nature. Then, at the end of the month, the installation is taken down, and the gravel is raked once more into a geometrical pattern.

Although the fourteenth-century Zen Buddhist monk Musō Soseki warned of the danger of mistaking artistic aims for spiritual goals, the human spirit will never stop seeking to express itself through art. The enthusiasm for gardens is as strong as it ever was in Musō's day.

THE SOUTH GARDEN OF THE *DAI-SHOIN* AT ŌBAI-IN

The south garden of the *dai-shoin* (large reception hall) building at the Daitoku-ji sub-temple Ōbai-in is said to have been created by the tea master Sen no Rikyū for the warlord Toyotomi Hideyoshi. It features a dry pond in the shape of a Japanese gourd with a piece of string tied around its middle. The gourd was the emblem that Hideyoshi used on his military pennants. The garden also includes a *sanzon-seki* (three sacred stones) arrangement, with a colossal central stone said to have been brought there from Mt Hiei by the first abbot of Daitoku-ji back in the early decades of the fourteenth century. This stone represents the Buddhist guardian spirit Fudō-myō'ō. Until very recently, the garden was quite densely planted with trees and shrubs, but these have been substantially thinned, changing the ambience of the garden considerably. The new buildings in the background are now visible, but this is as a result of a deliberate decision by the abbot of Ōbai-in.

LEFT The stone lantern in the foreground was brought to the south garden from Korea by Katō Kiyomasa, one of Toyotomi Hideyoshi's generals.

RIGHT This garden is traditionally said to have been designed by Sen no Rikyū for Toyotomi Hideyoshi. The dry pond, which is in the shape of a figure of eight, is thought to represent a *hyōtan* gourd – Hideyoshi's insignia. The stone bridge symbolises a cord tied around the gourd's middle.

PART TWO

SYMBOLS AND MOTIFS
IN JAPANESE ZEN GARDENS

SYMBOLS AND MOTIFS
IN JAPANESE ZEN GARDENS

While the idea of creating a landscape has always been the fundamental principle behind Japanese garden design, there has also been a long-standing tradition of incorporating specific imagery to convey religious and other culturally important references. Thus, Japanese Zen temple gardens employ a range of imagery taken from Buddhist cosmography and mythology, as well as from fables and allegorical stories. The auspicious images of the turtle and the crane – Daoist emblems of longevity – are also frequently encountered in Japanese temple gardens.

Such images tend to be rendered in an abstract style and are not always easy to read. For example, a cluster of stones representing the turtle is often integrated into the overall design of the garden in the form of an island in the garden pond. Its actual identity is likely to be hinted at in a somewhat tangential manner, perhaps by means of a rounded stone that suggests the animal's outstretched neck.

This section of the book looks at the major, as well as some of the more unusual, images found in Japanese Zen temple gardens. It will also examine the role of *shakkei* (borrowed landscape) in the design of gardens. Lastly, it will explore the important relationship between Zen temple gardens and Japanese tea gardens. Zen Buddhism teaches the importance of being truly aware of each transient moment of our fleeting lives. Similarly, the Japanese tea garden is designed to make guests set aside their worldly concerns and concentrate on the here and now. It is not surprising to find that some of the most memorable Zen temple gardens are at the same time tea gardens.

LEFT An exquisite composition in the east garden of the *hōjō* (abbot's hall) at Shinju-an represents a miniature mountain landscape.

PRECEDING PAGES A stone basin at Reikan-ji has a bamboo scoop for rinsing hands.

THE POND AND BRIDGE

At large Rinzai Zen Buddhist temples, there is often a formal rectangular pond located in front of the *sanmon* (main inner gateway), which faces the temple's *hon-dō* (sanctuary), otherwise known as the *butsu-den*. The pond will have a bridge leading across it to this gate. The archetypal *sanmon* has three entrances (symbolising deliverance from the Three Poisons — desire, anger, and ignorance) and two storeys — the top floor housing a statue of either the Gautama Buddha or the bodhisattva Kannon Bosatsu, accompanied by the Sixteen *Rakan* (a group of legendary holy men particularly venerated in Japanese Zen Buddhism). Examples of this type of pond can be seen in Kyōto at Myōshin-ji, Kennin-ji and Tenryū-ji. At all of these temples, the pond is named the Hōjō-chi (Pond of Freed Life).

A *hōjō-chi* was a pond in which fish rescued from fishermen were released as a symbolic gesture of mercy. At Tōfuku-ji, however, the pond in front of its imposing *sanmon* has a different name: Shion-chi (Pond of Far Thought). The pond and the *sanmon* symbolise the idea of crossing over from our present existence to nirvana, a state where all destructive mental states that arise from desire (greed), anger and ignorance (confusion) have been extinguished and all suffering is at an end.

A similar idea is reflected in the image of the *Niga-byakudō* (Two Rivers, White Road) of the Jōdo sect of Buddhism. The *Niga-byakudō* is represented by a river that is crossed by a narrow white path. On the right-hand side of the path, there are raging torrents; on the left side, the river is of flames. The torrents symbolise human greed and passion; the flames, anger. Gautama Buddha, the historical Buddha, stands on the near shore, which represents this present existence; the Amida Buddha, accompanied by the Kannon Bosatsu and the Seishi Bosatsu, preside over the farther shore, which symbolises Jōdo, Amida's paradise. The Amida Buddha calls to us, while Gautama Buddha encourages us to take the narrow path across the treacherous river to the Amida's paradise.

OPPOSITE Live fish were formerly bought from
fishermen and released into temple ponds in a special
ceremony to mark the sanctity of all life.

BELOW The pond in front of Tōfuku-ji's imposing
sanmon (main inner gateway) symbolises the human
soul's passage from a state of ignorance and suffering
to one of spiritual enlightenment. The gate, which took
twenty years to build, was completed in 1405.

Tenryū-ji no longer has a *sanmon* (main inner gateway), but its symbolic pond survives. It is planted with lotuses (*Nelumbo nucifera*), which were believed to grow in the pond in the centre of the Amida Buddha's paradise. In other parts of Asia, such as Sri Lanka, it is the water lily (*Nymphaea*) rather than the lotus that is associated with the Gautama Buddha.

The garden at Eihō-ji is traditionally said to have been designed by Musō Soseki. The gently arching bridge has been rebuilt many times over the centuries, and was last restored in 2009. A bridge of a similar design is thought to have once spanned a section of the pond in Musō's garden at Saihō-ji.

Jōdo was considered to be the abode of the Amida Buddha, an Enlightened Being existing outside human time and space. There, he was surrounded by the faithful, who were still on the path to enlightenment. Adherents of the Jōdo sect of Buddhism prayed to the Amida that they, too, might be reborn in this paradise so that they might be able to meditate at the foot of Buddha himself. Jōdo was envisaged as having a central lake overlooked by a gorgeous pavilion and sacred trees. It was depicted in religious paintings such as mandalas, and, from the tenth century onwards, many Buddhist temples modelled on the image of the Western Paradise were built by the Japanese aristocracy.

Zen Buddhism did not have quite the same interest in the Western Paradise as the Jōdo sect, for it concentrated on the aim of attaining enlightenment in this existence rather than pinning one's hopes on the next. Thus, the Buddha who is the focus of devotional worship in Japanese Zen Buddhist temples tends to be the Siddhartha Gautama (Gautama Buddha), otherwise known as Shakyamuni.

Nonetheless, Zen temple gardens were influenced by the earlier Jōdo-style pond garden. A pond with a bridge is the main feature of Eihō-ji, a Rinzai Zen Buddhist temple founded by Musō Soseki more than twenty years before he became abbot of Saihō-ji, Kyōto's Moss Temple. Eihō-ji is located not far from the urban sprawl of the town of Tajimi in Gifu prefecture, but when Musō first arrived there in 1313 with a group of his disciples it was a secluded spot deep in the mountains. He founded a hermitage, and, in the following years, he built a small temple dedicated to the Kannon Bosatsu and is said to have begun creating the temple garden.

The present Kannon-dō (Hall of the Kannon Bosatsu) faces south over a pond called the Garyū-chi (Pond of the Sleeping Dragon), which is spanned by a gracefully arching wooden bridge. The Eihō-ji garden, while not quite symbolising the desire to be reborn in Jōdo, expresses the wish to be freed of the passions and to 'cross over' to the Kannon Bosatsu. A bodhisattva, such as the Kannon, is a being who has not yet attained Buddha-hood, but maintains a link with humankind so as to act as a guide and protector to those who seek spiritual enlightenment. This is the reason why the *sanmon* (main inner gateway) sometimes houses a statue of the Kannon instead of the Gautama Buddha. There is a close affinity between the layout of the Eihō-ji garden and the pairing of the *sanmon* with a pond.

Tenryū-ji's *ryūmon-baku* shows the carp already halfway up the waterfall. The triangular boulder at the very top of the knoll is an *enzan-seki* (distant mountain stone), suggesting the presence of a faraway mountain behind the falls. The flat-surfaced monolith by the edge of the pond symbolises a curtain of water; it is 2m/7ft high and 110cm/3½ft wide, but only 12cm/5in thick.

THE *RYŪMON-BAKU*: THE DRAGON-GATE WATERFALL AND THE CARP-STONE

A frequently encountered image in Zen Buddhist temple gardens is a waterfall with a stone representing a carp attempting to swim upriver. This type of waterfall arrangement is known as a *ryūmon-baku* (dragon-gate waterfall). The image derives from a Chinese legend associated with a particularly steep gorge on the Yellow River, where the river cuts through Mt Lóngmén, which translates as 'Dragon Gate'. It was believed that the carp that succeeds in swimming up this pass is transformed into a mighty dragon.

The earliest surviving Japanese example of a *ryūmon-baku* is often said to be the dry waterfall in the garden of Tōkō-ji, a temple in Yamanashi prefecture. This temple is known for its close association with the eminent Chinese Chán Buddhist monk Lan-ch'i Tao-lung, known in Japan as Rankei Dōryū. Dōryū arrived in Japan in 1246, bringing with him the rigorous disciplined Chán Buddhism of the Línjì (Rinzai) school, which had risen to prominence in China during the Southern Song dynasty. Dōryū quickly won the confidence of Hōjō Tokiyori, the fifth regent of the Kamakura shogunate (and *de facto* ruler of the country), and in 1253 he was appointed the abbot of Tokiyori's newly founded temple in Kamakura – Kenchō-ji.

Dōryū refers to the legend of the carp and the Dragon Gate Falls in a set of instructions and precepts he issued to his disciples at Kenchō-ji. While the legend turns up in Chinese literature as an exhortation to hard work, so that one might rise in the world, Dōryū used it not in the context of worldly advancement but to warn his disciples of the immense difficulties that lay between them and spiritual enlightenment, and at the same time to encourage them to persevere.

Despite – or because of – his closeness to the centre of political power, Dōryū later had false accusations of treason levied against him. As a consequence, he was banished from Kamakura. In 1262, he travelled to the land of Kai (the modern-day prefecture of Yamanashi), where he re-established a neglected

temple in the town of Kōfu, converting it into a Zen Buddhist temple and renaming it Tōkō-ji. He is said to have remained there for three years, during which time he is supposed to have designed its garden and its waterfall. But no records survive indicating that Dōryū had anything to do with a temple garden.

The case of Tōkō-ji illustrates the dangers that beset attempts to interpret historic gardens. Nothing is actually known about who created the present garden at Tōkō-ji, or when, let alone the intentions of its designers. It is possible that the waterfall arrangement was never intended to suggest the idea of a carp swimming up a waterfall, and that its association with the legend came about only after Dōryū's reference to it in his book of precepts became widely known. On the other hand, the waterfall arrangement may have been designed as a *ryūmon-baku* (dragon-gate waterfall) and constructed sometime after Dōryū's day, as a kind of homage to the great Zen master. Extensive restoration work on the temple was carried out in the middle of the sixteenth century, and some garden historians date the entire layout of the current garden to around that time.

Both the waterfall at Nanzen-in (which has running water) and the dry waterfall at Saihō-ji (which does not) have been described as examples of the *ryūmon-baku*, although neither has a stone that can definitely be identified as a *rigyo-seki* (carp stone). Musō Soseki, who is thought to have designed the dry waterfall at Saihō-ji, had served previously as the abbot of Nanzen-ji, and in that capacity he would have lived at Nanzen-in and presumably seen the waterfall in its garden. But it is impossible to tell whether that waterfall in any way inspired him to create the waterfalls at Saihō-ji or Tenryū-ji. Indeed, there are theories that the Tenryū-ji garden was not designed by Musō at all, but by some unnamed garden architect, quite possibly from China. The *ryūmon-baku* (dragon-gate waterfall) at Tenryū-ji is presently dry, but an illustration of the garden in a guidebook to Kyōto, published in 1799, showed it with abundantly flowing water. There was, formerly, a bamboo conduit that fed water to the waterfall from a nearby wellspring. However, it is not known whether this configuration was part of the waterfall when it was first built or whether it was added sometime later.

There is a magnificent *ryūmon-baku* at the Rinzai Zen Buddhist temple Jōei-ji in the west town of Yamaguchi. It is not clear whether this waterfall was originally designed to have flowing water or not. It is now dry, but there are several ponds higher up the forested mountainside from which water may have once been drawn. This *ryūmon-baku* is actually in the form of a series of rocky cascades, either seven or five in number depending on how one counts them. The head of the waterfall can be just seen from the woodland path that encircles the slopes to the rear of the Jōei-ji garden: massive upright stones have been set together like a shocking gaping hole gashed into the side of the hill. It is an audacious arrangement. The eye then follows the course of the cascades, jumping from one dry rock pool to the next, all the way down the steep hillside to the pond. There, in the water, a single, large, wedge-shaped stone rises above the *Sagittaria* leaves, which resemble a dense field of green arrowheads. This is the carp-stone. It is as though the creature is holding its head high above the waterweeds and staring intently up the cascades.

A different view of the Jōei-ji waterfall – more atmospheric than dynamic – can be enjoyed from the other side of the pond. When the air is cool, a shifting mountain fog descends down the mountain slope and cloaks the waterfall in thick vapour. It then truly looks like a vision out of an ink-brush painting.

SHUMISEN

According to ancient Indian cosmological belief, a mountain stands in the centre of the world. This is Shumisen (Mt Sumeru). The mountain is surrounded by eight seas alternating with eight rings of mountains. This world view was shared by both Hinduism and Buddhism, and it arrived very early in Japan. The sixth- to seventh-century empress Suiko is said to have had a palace garden with an ornate bridge and a stone representing Shumisen. It is reported in historical texts that this garden was created for her by a Korean artisan. From the evidence that has survived (albeit in fragments) of other examples of Shumisen stones from that period, it is likely that the empress's stone was carved.

Later representations of Shumisen are not always obvious. Many temples preserve a tradition that a stone in their garden is supposed to stand for Shumisen. In the garden at Rokuon-ji (Kinkaku-ji), there is a famous stone set as an islet in the pond. This stone is known as a *kusen-hakkai-seki* (nine-mountains-eight-oceans stone). It is, therefore, supposed to symbolise Shumisen and its surrounding mountains and oceans. It is a rugged, curiously shaped stone, said to have been brought from China.

A fine example of a temple garden designed around the image of Shumisen is found at Manpuku-ji in the town of Masuda in Shimane prefecture. Although this is not a Buddhist temple of the Zen school, it was the family temple of the Masuda clan – the rulers of the former realm of Iwami. The renowned Zen monk-cum-artist Sesshū, who enjoyed the patronage of the lords of Iwami, is believed to have lodged there for a while. It is to him that the garden is traditionally attributed.

Manpuku-ji is located in a built-up area of the town. Its garden is modest in size, and is separated by a row of trees from surrounding houses. Yet this garden is designed to contain symbolically the whole of the Buddhist cosmos. It is dominated by a large, sloping grassy mound, surmounted by a peaked stone shaped somewhat like an arrowhead. This stone represents Shumisen. More stones have been set into the front of the grassy mound to suggest the eight mountain ranges with which Shumisen was believed to be surrounded.

OPPOSITE In the garden at Manpuku-ji in the town of Masuda in west Japan, Shumisen is intentionally represented by a small stone on top of a knoll to emphasise its remoteness. The flat rectangular stone in the foreground is the *reihai-seki*. There is a dry cascade to the right.

BELOW The monk Ikkyū Sōjun's mausoleum at Shūon-an looks south on to a landscape representing Shumisen. The flat *reihai-seki* in front of the mausoleum faces towards the Shumisen stone.

These stones are angular and weighty. They converge on the slope like a set of ridges, and they lead the eye in zigzag fashion to the summit of the mound. The Shumisen stone, by contrast, is a relatively small stone, deliberately chosen to give an idea of a vast mountain seen from an incalculably far distance. The stones are very white, and when the sunlight is strong they look blanched against the lush green grass. A pond extends around the foot of the mound. Across this pond, there is a flat stone set flush in the lawn. This is a *reihai-seki* (worship stone).

A similar combination of a *reihai-seki* and a Shumisen stone can be seen in the garden of the mausoleum of the eminent, fifteenth-century Rinzai Zen monk Ikkyū Sōjun. The mausoleum is located at Shūon-an, a temple in the modern town of Kyō-tanabe, 23 kilometres/14 miles south of the city of Kyōto. Sometime around 1456, Ikkyū revived a derelict temple called Myōshō-ji, which had originally been founded towards the end of the thirteen century by Nanpo Shōmyō, one of the founding fathers of the Rinzai school of Zen Buddhism in Japan. Ikkyū renamed the temple Shūon-an in thanksgiving for the teachings of the great Zen master. After Ikkyū was appointed abbot of Daitoku-ji in 1474 (when he was already eighty), he is said to have had himself carried to and fro between Shūon-an and Kyōto in a palanquin. He died in 1481 and was interred at Shūon-an.

The mausoleum looks out on to a gravelled, south-facing *kare-sansui* (dry-landscape) garden, believed to have been created in the fifteenth century. There is a gate in the middle of the south garden wall, but no path or stepping stones are laid in the white gravel between this gate and the mausoleum building. The garden is designed with pruned azaleas, taller shrubs and stones, the most prominent among them being a needle-like stone representing Shumisen. In front of the mausoleum, there is a flat *reihai-seki*, facing towards the Shumisen stone. This *reihai-seki* symbolises Ikkyū's spirit in eternal contemplation of the truth of Buddha's teachings.

THE *SANZON-SEKI*: THREE SACRED STONES

Arrangements of garden stones in groups of three seem to have been aesthetically pleasing to the Japanese from ancient times. Over the centuries, such arrangements came to be associated with the artistic convention of depicting Buddha flanked on either side by a bodhisattva, a composition known as the *sanzon* (Three Holies) style. Eventually, stones were being arranged in groups of three as a direct reference to Buddha and his attendants.

It is a matter of some disagreement whether early surviving examples of three-stone groupings were necessarily intended to have a religious significance. In the eleventh-century, garden-design manual the *Sakutei-ki*, the author (believed to have been the aristocrat Tachibana no Toshitsuna) described stones standing in the garden like 'three Buddhist statues'.

At Saihō-ji, there is an eye-catching cluster of three large boulders, which have been set into the bank of a long narrow island in the garden pond. These stones have traditionally been referred to as a *sanzon-seki* (three sacred stones) arrangement, although it is not known whether the monk Musō Soseki actually intended these stones to represent Buddha accompanied by two bodhisattvas. In any case, the naturalistic way in which the stones have been set, which makes them appear like natural outcrops of rocks, proved extremely influential in garden design and was much copied: for example, in the garden at the former shogun Ashikaga Yoshimitsu's late-fourteenth-century villa the Kitayama-dono, which after his death became Rokuon-ji (Kinkaku-ji).

The powerful *sanzon-seki* arrangement found at Rokuō-in near Tenryū-ji is possibly another of a very few examples that survived the Ōnin War. Rokuō-in was originally the one and only *tacchū* (sub-temple) of a vast Zen Buddhist temple called Hōdō-ji, which Ashikaga Yoshimitsu built next to Tenryū-ji near the river Katsura to the west of the city of Kyōto. A reference to the Rokuō-in garden, written in 1487, described it as having been the work of the Zen Buddhist monk Nin-anshu, who was a garden designer and a favourite of the sixth Ashikaga shogun (and Yoshimitsu's son) Yoshinori. Rokuō-in's bold *sanzon-seki* arrangement is quite unusual, in that all the stones are angled in such a way that they point in different directions. It is a tight grouping, yet the tallest stone is not the one towards the rear, but the one on the left-hand side. There is a *reihai-seki* (worship stone) in front of the group.

Since Rokuō-in belongs to a Zen school of Buddhism, it celebrates the Buddha in the form of the Gautama Buddha, and so its *sanzon-seki*, too, has been traditionally interpreted as representing the Gautama Buddha flanked by his attendant bodhisattvas, the Monju Bosatsu and the Fugen Bosatsu.

OPPOSITE The three-stone grouping on the south side of Naga-jima, the southernmost island of the pond garden at Saihō-ji, is one of the archetypal examples of a Japanese *sanzon-seki* arrangement.

BELOW This daring and idiosyncratic example of a *sanzon-seki* arrangement, in which the stones point in different directions, serves as the focal point in the south garden at Rokuō-in.

Three manifestations of Buddha are symbolised in the east garden of Kōmyō-in, two of which (in the form of two *sanzon-seki* sacred stone arrangements) can be seen here. The rest of the stones represent rays of light emanating from the Buddhas. The gravel 'sea' is designed, unusually, to hold water after a rainstorm, to create a small pond.

In the case of the Myōshin-ji sub-temple Tōkai-an, the association of its *sanzon-seki* (three sacred stones) arrangement with the triad composition in Buddhist art is much more overt. Its two *shoin* (reception hall) gardens were created in 1814 by the Zen Buddhist monk Tōboku Sōho, who also made a woodblock plan of the gardens. This plan, which is still carefully preserved at Tōkai-an, showed the names that Tōboku Sōho had given to particular stones. In the west garden, there is a group of three stones, the central one of which is named the Shugo-seki (Guardian Stone). The stone on its right is called the Nitten-seki, and the one on the left the Gatten-seki. Nitten and Gatten refer to the Hindu sun-god and moon-god respectively; these deities were adopted by Buddhism as divine guardian beings.

The manifestation of Buddha known as the Yakushi-nyorai (in the West, referred to as the Medicine Buddha) is traditionally shown attended by a pair of bodhisattvas called the Nikkō Bosatsu (Bodhisattva of the Sunlight) and Gakkō Bosatsu (Bodhisattva of the Moonlight). Just as the Nitten-seki in the Tōkai-an garden is set on the right-hand side of the Guardian Stone and the Gatten-seki in on its left, the Bodhisattva of the Sunlight conventionally stands on the Buddha's right (when viewed from the front), while the Bodhisattva of the Moonlight is on the left.

This composition is subtly reflected in the garden at Daisen-in, the Daitoku-ji sub-temple with the famous *kare-sansui* (dry-landscape) garden. The dry-waterfall arrangement, which stands at the heart of the garden, has ancient camellia shrubs planted around it. To its right, there is a camellia with anemone-form, red flowers, called 'Jikkō' ('Daylight'), while on its left there is another camellia with anemone-form, red, single flowers that have white petaloids, called 'Gakkō' ('Moonlight').

There is no doubt whatsoever that the three *sanzon-seki* arrangements in Shigemori Mirei's 1939 Hashin-tei (Garden of the Moonlight on the Waves), which he created for Kōmyō-in, a *tacchū* (sub-temple) of Tōfuku-ji, have a religious significance. The name of the garden is a reference to a Zen Buddhist saying to the effect that 'the moon which rises in a cloudless sky shines its light on the waves.' Shigemori uses gravel and moss to symbolise the sea and the land, and pebbles to represent salt spray lashed on the beach. There are three *sanzon-seki* arrangements in this garden: they stand for the Gautama Buddha, the Amida Buddha and the Yakushi-nyorai, respectively, each with their attendant bodhisattvas. Together, they form one large *sanzon* (Three Holies) composition. The rest of the stones in the garden are subtly arranged to represent beams of light emanating in all directions from the three Buddhas – this is a direct reference to the name of the sub-temple, for *kōmyō* is the Japanese term for the light that emerges from Buddha, symbolising Buddha's wisdom and mercy.

The *hōjō* (abbot's hall) and two *shoin* (reception hall) buildings face out on to Shigemori's garden Hashin-tei, and they form its west and north boundaries. On its east side, there is a sharp incline thickly planted with azaleas, which Shigemori turned into a bank clipped to represent clouds. In the Zen saying from which the garden takes its name, these cloud-shrubs symbolise earthly passions and carnal desires. The azaleas, some of which are Satsuki azaleas while others are Tsutsuji varieties, were collected from all over Japan by Yokomaku Tekisen, who had become abbot of Kōmyō-in in 1911. He had found the place in a deplorable state of dilapidation, owing to the anti-Buddhist upheavals of the late 1860s and 1870s, and he spent more than twenty years collecting alms for the temple restoration. In 1939, he asked Shigemori Mirei, who was working on the *hōjō* garden for the main temple at Tōfuku-ji, whether he could not do something for his *tacchū*. As well as constructing the Hashin-tei, Shigemori returned to Kōmyō-in in 1957, to build a teahouse, and again in 1962, to create a smaller garden near the front entrance. This garden, too, features a *sanzon-seki*: it stands astride the back of a symbolic turtle.

THE CHŌ'ON-TEI, KENNIN-JI

A beautiful contemporary use of the *sanzon-seki* (three sacred stones) arrangement can be seen in the Chō'on-tei (Garden of the Sound of the Sea) at Kennin-ji. This garden, completed in 2006, was designed by the garden architect Kitayama Yasuo in conjunction with Kobori Tai'gan, the 487th abbot of Kennin-ji. Surrounded on all four sides by the *dai-shoin* (large reception hall), the *ko-shoin* (small reception hall) and the two corridors that connect them, it is a beautiful courtyard garden designed to be viewed from every direction. The ground is contoured so it subtly suggests the land and the sea, although this garden does not use gravel to represent water. Kitayama conceived the design of the Chō'on-tei in terms of a loose spiral, in the centre of which stand the three stones comprising the *sanzon-seki*. The outer curve of the spiral is indicated by a flat-topped *zazen* (sitting meditation) stone.

Kennin-ji's Chō'on-tei is designed to be viewed from all directions, so that there is no single 'front' or 'rear' to the garden: the view from the *ko-shoin* (small reception hall) towards the south-west corner of the *dai-shoin* (top left); the view from the *dai-shoin* with the *zazen* stone to the far right (below left); the view from the south-west corner of the *dai-shoin* with a superb *Enkianthus perulatus* with its autumn foliage in the foreground (right).

THE KANNON AND FUDŌ STONES

While the *sanzon-seki* (three sacred stones) arrangement is very popular and is frequently encountered across Japan, several gardens at Daitoku-ji possess a more unusual, two-stone arrangement as their focal point. The archetype is at Daisen-in, where there are two standing stones that look almost like hands held up together in prayer. These stones have traditionally been identified with two sacred Buddhist entities: the Kannon Bosatsu (the bodhisattva who is associated with mercy) and Fudō-myō'ō (the fierce and fiery guardian of truth). There has not, however, been a consensus about which stone symbolises which. In the south garden of Daitoku-ji's *dai-hōjō* (large hall), its dry waterfall takes the unusual form of two stone slabs standing side by side. These, too, have been associated with the Kannon Bosatsu and Fudō-myō'ō: the former with the right-hand stone, and the latter with the stone on the left.

A third garden possesses a pairing of stones, but is completely different in style. This is the south garden of the *hon-dō* (sanctuary), formerly known as the *kyaku-den* (guest hall) at Ōbai-in, another of Daitoku-ji's many sub-temples. Ōbai-in was founded in the sixteenth century, but appears to have been rebuilt several times during the same century. Its *kuri* (domestic quarters) date back to 1589, and it is the oldest extant building of its type in Japan. It once housed up to seventy novice monks.

Ōbai-in's *hon-dō* is laid out very much in the manner of the traditional Zen temple *hōjō* (abbot's hall), and its three public rooms – the *shicchū* (central room) with a formal reception room on either side of it – face south on to a walled garden. This garden, which is believed to have been created towards the end of the sixteenth century, is distinguished by the startling simplicity of its design. Approximately two-thirds of it is laid only with raked white gravel, which symbolises the ocean. The remaining third, which stretches along the rear garden wall, is carpeted with moss, and represents land. The two sections are separated by a thin row of white edging stones. Some garden historians south garden of Ōbai-in's *hon-dō* (sanctuary) have the appearance of two people in deep conversation (far right); a *Stewartia pseudocamellia* is grouped with a flat stone, symbolising a devout follower bowing to Buddha (right); the upright Fudō stone on the left is set so that it tapers towards to the ground, making it resemble a standing human figure (below right).

see this row of edging stones as a reference to the image of the *Niga-byakudō*, the narrow path that crosses the treacherous river of torrents and of flames and leads to the Amida Buddha's paradise.

Standing in the moss towards the west end of the garden are two large stones with only a single tiny shrub between them. At the other end, a flat stone lies buried in the moss under a deciduous camellia (*Stewartia pseudocamellia*). The standing stones and the tree are silhouetted against the garden wall behind them. This wall acts as a sort of blank canvas, and the effect is reminiscent of the *zanzan jōsui* style of ink-brush painting, in which most of the picture is left unfilled. The two upright stones are situated directly in front of the west reception room. As in the case of the stones in both the Daisen-in garden and the south garden of Daitoku-ji's *dai-hōjō* (large hall), the right-hand stone in the Ōbai-in arrangement is known as the Kannon stone, while the one on the left has been associated either with the Fudō-myō'ō or the Seishi Bosatsu (the Kannon Bosatsu's traditional partner in Japanese Buddhist art when accompanying the Amida Buddha).

The stones seem to lean towards each other, as though they were two figures in deep conversation. For this reason, the pair is also thought to represent a Zen master instructing his disciple, and is called the Chōmon-seki (Sermon Stones). The stones have been identified with two of the Gautama Buddha's ten main disciples – the taller with Maka-kashō (who became the first Buddhist patriarch after the Gautama Buddha) and the other, which resembles a kneeling figure, with Ananda (who became the second patriarch). The *Stewartia pseudocamellia* and its accompanying stone at the other end of the garden are said to symbolise the Gautama Buddha with a worshipper at his feet.

LEFT The turtle island in the pond garden at Rokuon-ji (Kinkaku-ji) can be distinguished from the adjacent crane one by its triangular stone resembling a turtle's raised head. The jagged stone to the left of the crane island is famous as the *kusen-hakkai-seki* (nine-mountains-eight-oceans stone), symbolising Shumisen and its surrounding mountains.

RIGHT This delicate **example** of a crane island is to be found at Saihō-ji.

DAOIST IMAGERY: THE CRANE, THE TURTLE AND THE ISLANDS OF THE IMMORTALS

The image of the crane and the turtle as symbols of longevity and good fortune comes from Daoist tradition. Daoism, a series of philosophical and religious beliefs that originated in China, arrived early in Japan. There is a Japanese saying that the crane lives a thousand years and the turtle, ten thousand. Although it is not certain when they first began to be represented in Japanese gardens, both the crane and the turtle were certainly becoming a popular feature by the eleventh century. The earliest surviving, Japanese, garden-design manual, the *Sakutei-ki*, which dates from that century, recommended that garden ponds should be 'dug in the shape of a turtle or a crane'. The *Sakutei-ki* concerned itself with aristocratic gardens of the *shinden-zukuri* style, and it is clear that the turtle and crane were considered suitably auspicious images for a palace garden, and were already being represented, moreover, in a highly stylised way.

It is, therefore, not surprising that they make an appearance in the pond garden at Rokuon-ji (Kinkaku-ji), seeing as this garden was originally built towards the end of the fourteenth century as a palace garden for Ashikaga Yoshimitsu. There, the creatures take the form of islands: for example, the pair of small islands in front of the Kinkaku (Golden Pavilion) stands for the crane and turtle. They are both planted with a pine tree, which is, also, an auspicious symbol of longevity. The turtle is quite literally depicted, with a semi-upright stone at one end, representing its head, and other stones symbolising its flippers and tail. Because of the proximity of these two islands, it is probable that the long narrow island close by, which is called Ashihara-jima after a mythological name for Japan, was also meant to suggest Mt Hōrai, one of the Islands of the Immortals. There are several more turtle islands located around the lake: they are similarly identifiable by their tilted heads, and one has a large squat boulder representing its shell.

If it is correct that the elaborate stone arrangements in the sixteenth-century Daisen-in garden at Daitoku-ji originally came from a palace garden belonging to a high-ranking Kyōto family, this might explain the presence of the turtle and the crane. Again, they take the form of islands, but, since this is a dry garden, the water is symbolised by raked gravel. The crane island is distinguishable by a prominent triangular stone and a jagged upright boulder, which represent its wings, while a flat stone symbolises its tail. The turtle island incorporates stones variously representing its head, a flipper and a part of its carapace. This last stone, a flat-topped boulder, is also known as the Zazen-seki (Meditation Stone), although its presence there is more symbolic than practical. The craggy upright wing stone of the crane island has acquired the name Daruma-seki (Dharma Stone), after Bodhidharma, the Indian monk said to have introduced Chán (Zen) Buddhism to China and who, according to legend, sat meditating for nine consecutive years.

Chinese Buddhism was deeply influenced by Daoism, with its emphasis on freedom from illusion and detachment from the passions. It embraced Daoism's advocacy of a simple life in accordance with the essential principles of the natural world. It also shared the Daoist view that a human being should aim to be at one with nature but, at the same time, remain above it – that is, not be subject to its limitations. The Eight Immortals (legendary Daoist sages who were believed to live on Mt Hōrai) and Seven Sages of the Bamboo Grove (a group of supposedly third-century Chinese scholars and artists who retired to a life of rural seclusion dedicated to philosophical debate) both became popular subjects for Japanese *fusuma* (sliding partition-wall) paintings for the *hōjō* (abbot's hall).

Taizō-in – one of the oldest of Myōshin-ji's forty-eight sub-temples – has a famous *kare-sansui* (dry-landscape) garden with a turtle-and-crane theme. This garden has traditionally been attributed to the important Japanese artist Kanō Motonobu, who had a career that stretched from the last decades of the fifteenth century to the middle of the sixteenth. Motonobu is credited with having applied elements of traditional Japanese painting – particularly the use of colour – to the ink-brush painting techniques that had come to Japan from China. He was instrumental in developing painting styles for decorating *fusuma* (sliding partition walls) and *byōbu* (standing screens). He produced sets of *fusuma* paintings for several temples, including the *hōjō* (abbot's hall) at Daisen-in in 1513. In 1543, he painted a series for Reiun-in, the high-ranking sub-temple of Myōshin-ji. Motonobu practised meditation under the guidance of the monk Daikyū Sōkyū, who lived at Reiun-in, and his paintings were executed as part of his daily devotional regime.

Taizō-in was moved to its current site within the grounds of Myōshin-ji sometime during the 1520s or 1530s by Ki'nen Zenyū, who was a disciple of Reiun-in's Daikyū Sōkyū and later became the thirty-eighth abbot of Myōshin-ji. It is believed that the garden at Taizō-in was built during the lifetime of Ki'nen Zenyū, whose death occurred in the winter of 1561–2. One suggestion is that it was created as part of the commemorations, held in 1559, marking the 200th anniversary of the death of Myōshin-ji's founding abbot. Since the artist Kanō Motonobu did not die until 1559, it is theoretically possible that he could have participated in the design of the garden. It is also feasible that Motonobu knew the famous *kare-sansui* (dry-landscape) garden at Reiun-in, which had been created sometime before 1549 for the emperor Go-Nara. On the other hand, the Taizō-in garden could very well predate Reiun-in's garden.

Despite all of these tantalising possibilities, there is a frustrating lack of concrete information. It is not even certain whether the garden, which is located on the west side of Taizō-in's *hōjō*, was erected for the present building. There is a temple tradition that a new *hōjō* was put up sometime during the fifty years following Ki'nen Zenyū's death. It may be that this *hōjō* was constructed next to an existing garden or that a garden was made specifically for this building. If the latter, it would make the creation of the Taizō-in garden even more recent.

It is not surprising, however, that this garden has been attributed to an admired artist, for the experience of viewing it is very like viewing a set of *fusuma* (sliding partition-wall) paintings. While the scene depicted on each *fusuma* can be appreciated on its own, the entire set of *fusuma* constitutes one vast composition. Likewise, each section of the Taizō-in garden is very detailed, but it is only when one's eyes have slowly travelled the whole length of the garden that its full scope can be appreciated. While there is a certain severity and grandeur about the *kare-sansui* garden at Daisen-in, for example, where the Kannon and Fudō stones suggest the craggy mountain peaks found in the most stately of Chinese landscape painting styles, Taizō-in's *kare-sansui* garden represents a gentler landscape, more calming than awe-inspiring. Unusually, it occupies a semi-circular site, and at its centre there is an oval pond laid with white gravel. In the far right-hand corner is a dry waterfall. The pebbles, representing the current, draw the visitor's eyes down the waterfall and towards the central pond and its island, which takes the shape of a turtle. This island is connected to the banks of the pond by two stone bridges, one of which serves also as the turtle's tail. On the far side of the dry pond, there is a large stone representing Mt Hōrai in the distance.

An imaginary current flows around the sides of the turtle island, to the left of which there is a single narrow stone, its tapering shape suggesting the speed of the current. Because this stone also resembles the dorsal fin of a swimming fish, it is known as the *funa-ishi* (*funa*-fish stone) – *funa* being a common Japanese freshwater fish. Close by, another fine stone rises proudly like a promontory jutting out on to a lake. Beyond it is a triangular stone, representing the raised wing of a crane in flight.

At the far left edge of the garden, the gravel pond splits into two. One branch continues under a bridge comprising a single slab of stone. The other passes in front of a row of stones representing a faraway mountain range (which includes a stone resembling Mt Fuji in shape) and around

the corner of the *hōjō* (abbot's hall), towards the building's moss-covered south garden, which is planted with a Japanese red pine (*Pinus densiflora*).

Many striking turtle-and-crane gardens were created in the seventeenth century, but perhaps none as imposing in scope as those dedicated to powerful warlords such as Toyotomi Hideyoshi and Tokugawa Ieyasu. For example, the turtle and the crane constitute the central imagery of the pond garden at Kōdai-ji, a magnificent temple founded by Hideyoshi's widow O'ne in his memory. They are also the theme of the *kare-sansui* (dry-landscape) garden at Konchi-in, Kobori Enshū's grand homage to the ascendancy of the Tokugawa dynasty. Interestingly, there is an old tradition that the pond garden at Kōdai-ji, too, was created by Enshū, whose father had once been an adviser to Hideyoshi's brother.

BELOW This view of the stone representing a crane's wing is seen against the moon-viewing platform of Kōdai-ji's west bridge and the Kaisan-dō; the turtle island is on the north side of the west bridge (bottom).

OPPOSITE A view of Kōdai-ji's *hōjō* (abbot's hall) from the Kaisan-dō, with the crane's wing stone in the middle distance.

KŌDAI-JI

This temple was founded in 1606 by Toyotomi Hideyoshi's widow O'ne (usually known by her title Kita-no-mandokoro) in memory of her husband and her adoptive parents. The temple suffered four catastrophic fires over the centuries, but the pond garden survived. Its two ponds lie on either side of the Kaisan-dō, a shrine dedicated to O'ne's brother, where O'ne herself is buried. Roofed bridges lead from the building across the ponds. The bridge on the west side has an elegant shingled pavilion from which it used to be possible to view the moon in the sky or its reflection in the water. There are stones around this pond representing the crane and the turtle. On the other side of the Kaisan-dō, a roofed bridge called the Ga'ryō-rō (Corridor of the Recumbent Dragon) spans the east pond and extends up the hillside to another shrine, the sumptuous Otama-ya, dedicated to the memory of Hideyoshi and O'ne. Kōdai-ji initially belonged to the Sōtō school of Japanese Zen Buddhism, but changed to the Rinzai Zen school in accordance with O'ne's wishes a few months before her death in 1624.

LEFT The full scope of the historic *kare-sansui* (dry-landscape) garden at Entoku-in is best appreciated from the south-west corner of the *shoin* (reception hall).

BELOW LEFT The weighty middle bridge links the garden's two islands at Entoku-in. Beyond it, the garden's dry waterfall can be seen on the left, while the Shumisen arrangement with surrounding mountains is situated up the slope to the right. The Shumisen stone itself is partly hidden here by a Japanese maple branch.

Another celebrated example of a turtle-and-crane garden is found at Entoku-in, a sub-temple of Kōdai-ji. The site was the former residence of the eldest brother of Toyotomi Hideyoshi's widow O'ne. Her dressing hall from Fushimi Castle had been brought there, and she bequeathed the building to her nephew, who converted it into a small Buddhist temple. Later, in 1632, he established a family temple on the premises, naming it Entoku-in. It is astonishing to think that the temple is located around the corner from the geisha houses and the exclusive restaurants of the Gion district of Kyōto.

There are two theories about the origins of the garden: one is that it was created by O'ne's nephew, and the other that the stones were brought from Fushimi Castle and reassembled there in front of O'ne's dressing hall. The latter theory would account for the sheer opulence (and size) of the stones, with their subtle range of colours, shapes and textures. The sense of history and the knowledge of the eventual demise of the Toyotomi clan give an added poignancy to this garden. At the same time, its presence in a Zen temple garden lends it a majesty that is beyond the worldly vanity of the rich and powerful.

The composition of the garden is very traditional, yet the design is bold. It fills the compact site without overcrowding it. O'ne's

RIGHT This bridge is composed of three cut-stone slabs balanced delicately on a stone pier. A *sanzon-seki* (three sacred stones) arrangement can be seen under the branches of the Japanese maple on the opposite side of the bridge.

BELOW RIGHT The triangular stones suggest this island represents the crane; the stone under the pine tree, however, has been interpreted as symbolising the turtle's carapace.

dressing hall no longer exists, and a different *shoin* (reception hall) building now stands in its place, but the 'L'-shaped, dry pond garden, which was created around the north-east corner of O'ne's building, still survives.

This is a garden that sets out to impress. It features two islands representing the turtle and the crane, but what dominate the composition are three massive stone bridges, which connect the islands with each other, as well as to the banks of the pond. All three bridges are very different in character. Two comprise hefty slabs of natural stone, and yet one of them exudes a certain airiness, as though it were effortlessly spanning a great gulf, while the other slab, consisting of two weightier blocks, needs to be propped up with more stones wedged underneath them. The bridge on the far right is made up of three delicate cut stones, which give it an altogether ethereal feel. These bridges constitute the heads and tails of the turtle and crane, which are represented by the two islands.

The rear of the pond garden at Entoku-in has been built up to create a slope, and there is a dry waterfall arrangement leading down to the pond. Some garden historians have hypothesised that the pond has not always been dry, and that the waterfall had originally been designed to have running water, which fed the pond. Others

OPPOSITE TOP The turtle's head on the right and the crane's neck on the left form the view from the main reception room of the *hōjō* at Funda-in (left); the crane and turtle islands are seen here against clipped evergreens and woodland (right).

OPPOSITE BOTTOM The turtle bears a wedged-shaped stone on its back symbolising Mt Hōrai (left); a view of the Ekan-dō teahouse and a section of the east *hōjō* garden with Shigemori Mirei's own crane island, and a cluster of stones to its right symbolising the Islands of the Immortals (right).

disagree. In any event, the kidney-shaped pond is now dry, and the pond bed is covered in moss. On the slope behind the right-hand bridge with its cut-stone slabs, there is a *sanzon-seki* (three sacred stones) arrangement, on the left of which (on the other side of a Japanese maple) stands a broad, triangular Shumisen boulder with a ring of stones around it.

The image of the turtle and the crane lies at the heart of one particularly fascinating historical puzzle that concerns the south garden of the *hōjō* (abbot's hall) at Funda-in, a sub-temple of Tōfuku-ji. According to the traditions of the sub-temple, the celebrated fifteenth-century artist–monk Sesshū not only stayed there whenever he visited Tōfuku-ji, but also designed this garden. In 1937, Shigemori Mirei surveyed it and concluded on stylistic grounds that it must indeed have been created by Sesshū; that it had consisted of two stone groups, one representing the crane and the other the turtle; and that it dated back to sometime before 1467, the year in which the Ōnin War started. The Funda-in garden is a *kare-sansui* (dry-landscape) garden, which employs gravel to indicate water. Shigemori's dating would make it one of the earliest surviving examples of this type of garden. In 1939, Shigemori undertook the restoration of the garden, basing his decisions on his survey and on survey work he had conducted at another temple garden traditionally attributed to Sesshū – the one at Jōei-ji in the town of Yamaguchi in west Japan.

The attribution of the Funda-in garden to Sesshū is problematical, because no documentation exists attesting that Sesshū ever stayed at Tōfuku-ji or at any of its sub-temples, let alone designed a garden for one of them. Then there is the separate question of whether Shigemori would have had all of the original garden stones at his disposal, seeing that the shogun Ashikaga Yoshimasa is recorded as having ordered, in the autumn of 1460, ten garden stones and a tree to be removed from the garden at Funda-in and taken to a garden that was being built for a residential hall at Shōkoku-ji – a prestigious Zen Buddhist temple founded by Yoshimasa's grandfather. This raises the question as to whether the garden that has survived is essentially the one from which the ten stones were plundered or whether it is a different garden that was created anew after that event. Besides, who is to say that more stones did not go missing during or after the Ōnin War?

The Funda-in garden as it now stands can be characterised as a tranquil, rather than a challenging, garden. Its distinctive atmosphere owes much to its rich greenery, which displays hues ranging from the cool blue-greens of the conifers through to the ruddy tones of the new growth on the photinia. The sculpted evergreen specimen trees present a striking contrast to the lush mixed woodland, which serves as a backdrop for the entire garden. In front of the *hōjō*, there is a small area of raked gravel signifying a pond. The two groupings of stone, representing the turtle and the crane respectively, do not take the form of islands in the pond, but are found on the moss beyond the gravelled area. They take the form of shoreline boulders, rather than rocky islands in the middle of the pond.

There are two stone clusters. The one on the right is composed of two concentric rings encircling a low mound, which is surmounted by a single, blade-shaped stone. One might be forgiven for thinking at first sight that this conspicuous stone vaguely resembles the spread-out wing of a crane. But this grouping actually represents the turtle, with the concentric rings suggesting its shell. The explanation given for the presence of an upright stone on the turtle's back is that it stands for Mt Hōrai. The left-hand stone cluster might look more turtle-like than the other, since it is mainly of low, horizontally set stones. It, however, symbolises the crane with an outstretched neck. The turtle, too, has a head; it is the small nobbly rock sticking out of the lower ring of stones in the right-hand cluster. The two creatures face each other with a diminutive azalea between them. Shigemori has sited them in such a way that when one sits in the main reception room of the *hōjō*, the garden view is of

an auspicious image: the heads of the crane and turtle turned harmoniously towards each other.

It has to be said that the stones in this garden at Funda-in do not have the dynamic quality of the stones found in other gardens attributed to Sesshū, although this does not, in itself, constitute enough of an argument against attributing the garden to Sesshū. Apart from the quality of the stones, some of Shigemori's critics have not been persuaded that what Shigemori did with them reflects anything of Sesshū's artistic style or flair. An unresolved question is whether this garden, for all its charm, would have become quite as famous as it now is, were it not for its association with Sesshū. Ultimately, the garden has to be appreciated according to its own merits, but this is rather more difficult to do than one might expect.

THE ISSHIDAN GARDEN, RYŌGEN-IN SUB-TEMPLE, DAITOKU-JI

Ryōgen-in, one of the sub-temples of Daitoku-ji, possessed two historic gardens, one on the south side of the *hōjō* (abbot's hall), and the other on the north. The south *hōjō* garden, called the Isshidan, formerly featured a Chinese *Camellia sasanqua* said to have been more than 700 years old. Named after Yáng Guìfēi (the famous beauty who became the consort of the Chinese emperor Xuánzōng), it produced scarlet flowers throughout the winter months. This tree died in the spring of 1980, and the abbot at the time decided to make use of the opportunity to create an altogether new garden. The Isshidan is now a *hira-niwa* (flat garden) symbolising the ocean, with three 'islands': a turtle island, a crane island and Mt Hōrai. The success of this garden is due to the marvellous choice of stones and the bold simplicity of their layout.

The sloping roof of Ōbai-in's *hon-dō* (sanctuary) serves as a backdrop to Ryōgen-in's Isshidan garden, which is dominated by an imposing, oval-shaped turtle island (below); the Mt Hōrai stone, with the crane island in the foreground, seen from the south-west corner of Ryōgen-in's *hōjō* (abbot's hall) (top left); the stones symbolising Mt Hōrai and the other two Islands of the Immortals have been planted with ornamental grasses and ferns (below left).

The curved roofline of the Ga'ryō-rō (Corridor of the Recumbent Dragon) is reflected in the east pond of Kōdai-ji's historic garden. The corridor extends up the hillside, linking the Kaisan-dō (a shrine dedicated to O'ne's brother), glimpsed on the far left, with another shrine, dedicated to Toyotomi Hideyoshi and his wife O'ne.

THE DRAGON

The dragon has traditionally had a special place in Chinese culture. The blue dragon was one of four supernatural creatures, each of which was believed to preside over one of the four quadrants of the compass. The dragon symbolised nature's power to transform itself: it was said to dwell deep underwater during the autumn and to climb to heaven in spring. It was believed to live underground as well as in the sea. The roar of a dragon summoned thunder clouds, tempests and rain. Rain could be very beneficial, of course, but, if the dragon was angered, it caused flooding. The dragon sometimes manifested itself in the shape of water spouts and cyclones. It carried a round jewel, either under its chin or in its claws. This stone is sometimes described as a flaming gem that is red in colour, while according to other legends it is a lustrous pearl.

It has variously been explained as a symbol of the sun (because the dragon presides over the east) or as the source of the dragon's power. The sound of thunder is said to be produced when the dragon rolls this jewel. According to Daoist mythology, there were four dragon kings who ruled over the four oceans of the universe and controlled clouds, rain and thunder. The dragon was also the Chinese emblem of imperial authority.

The *nāga*, a serpent-shaped supernatural being, entered Buddhist legends from Hindu mythology. A *nāga* in the form of a king cobra with seven heads was supposed to have shielded Siddhartha Gautama from the elements as he sat in meditation. When Buddhism reached China, the Indian *nāga* got conflated with the Chinese dragon. In Japan, the dragon assumed the role of defender of the Buddhist religion. Because it was associated with rain, the dragon

The stones and clipped azaleas in the north garden of the *hōjō* at Ryōgen-in are said to resemble the figure of a dragon with a raised head, an extended claw and a round jewel with which dragons were associated. The tree in the far corner is a holly, *Ilex rotunda*.

became linked with the life-giving teachings of Buddha, which, it was said, are showered on all humankind. Paintings of dragons often embellished the *hōjō* (abbot's hall) and *hattō* (lecture hall) of temples of the Rinzai Zen school, for these were the buildings in which Buddha's teachings were imparted by the master to his disciples.

Surprisingly, dragons do not appear very frequently in the temple garden, although the south pond at Nanzen-in is said to be in the shape of a coiled dragon. The dramatic roofed bridge that links two of the temple buildings at Kōdai-ji is named the Ga'ryō-rō (Corridor of the Recumbent Dragon), and the pond it spans is called the Ga'ryō-chi (Pond of the Recumbent Dragon).

The dragon is one of the interpretations given to the stone arrangement in the north garden of the *hōjō* at Ryōgen-in, one of the oldest surviving *tacchū*

(sub-temples) of Daitoku-ji. Its six-chambered *hōjō* dates from the beginning of the sixteenth century, and is one of the earliest existing examples of its type. The north garden is something of a mystery. There are no records to suggest when it might have been created or by whom, although there is a tradition that it was designed by the shogun Ashikaga Yoshimasa's art expert, Sōami, who was active towards the end of the fifteenth century and the beginning of the sixteenth.

The garden at Ryōgen-in appears to have remained all but forgotten until Shigemori Mirei wrote about it in 1933. It is a rectangular courtyard extending the whole length of the *hōjō*. As is the case with the *hōjō* at Daisen-in – that other ancient sub-temple of Daitoku-ji – the *shoin* (formal study) occupies the north-east corner of the *hōjō* building. But whereas the Daisen-in *shoin* faces eastwards, the Ryōgen-in *shoin* (formal study) looks out diagonally on to the north garden. A long garden wall separates this garden from the grounds of the sub-temple next door. There is a camellia in the north-east corner, and a tall, venerable-looking holly tree (*Ilex rotunda*) at the west end. Unlike the south garden of the *hōjō* (abbot's hall), the north garden is completely carpeted in moss. Between the camellia and the *Ilex rotunda*, and against the backdrop created by the plastered garden wall, stones have been set among cropped azalea bushes. The selection of stones indicates that a great deal of effort was involved in the creation of this garden, for the material is expensive *aoishi* (chlorite schist) brought all the way from the island of Shikoku. They are not large, but well balanced in size and shape so that they complement each other exquisitely.

Conspicuous among these stones is a tall vertical one that leans to the right. It would look unstable if it were not for the smaller stones that flank it on either side – two to the left and one to the right. The Satsuki azaleas, which have been planted among these stones, have grown into large cushions, and these also help to soften the feeling of precariousness about this stone cluster.

Several explanations have been given for this unusual configuration in the north garden of the *hōjō* at Ryōgen-in. One is that it is an incomplete dry waterfall that has lost several of its constituent stones. Another is that it takes the form of a *sanzon-seki* (three sacred stones), with the central leaning stone symbolising Shumisen, the mountain at the centre of the Buddhist universe. The round stone in front of it would be the *reihai-seki* (worship stone), with the other stones and azaleas in the garden representing the eight mountain ranges with which Shumisen is surrounded. The moss symbolises the eight oceans. Perhaps the most ingenious interpretation – which by no means negates the previous ones – is that the stones represent a dragon with its head raised so that it is facing anyone sitting in the *shoin*. The other stones and pruned azaleas farther down the garden then become sections of the

dragon's writhing body protruding above the waves – or perhaps above the clouds. The flat round stone lying among the moss in the foreground would be the precious jewel that dragons are depicted grasping between their claws.

The north garden of Ryōgen-in's *hōjō* is called the Ryōgin-tei (Garden of the Roaring Dragon). It shares this name with the west garden of Ryōgin-an, an ancient sub-temple at Tōfuku-ji.

Ryōgin-an was founded in 1291 by the third abbot of Tōfuku-ji Mukan Fumon, who, towards the end of his life, also became the first abbot of Nanzen-ji. Ryōgin-an was intended as his residence, but he died there the year in which it was built, and, after his death, it became a *tacchū* (sub-temple) of Tōfuku-ji. Despite its history, Ryōgin-an became neglected after the anti-Buddhist troubles of the late 1860s and early 1870s. Its *hōjō*, which dates back to *c*.1387 and is in an earlier style than the example now seen at Ryōgen-in, was finally restored in 1964. It was then that the garden historian and architect Shigemori Mirei removed the scrub and the vegetable beds with which the building had become surrounded and created three brand-new gardens.

These three gardens are located on the south, east and west sides of the *hōjō* respectively. The building faces south in the traditional manner, and Shigemori laid this garden with white gravel, leaving it flat and unadorned after the ancient custom of having a cleared ceremonial space in front of the *hōjō*. He did, however, design a bamboo fence to partition the south garden from the west garden. This fence is decorated with a pattern of zigzagged thunderbolts, which anticipates the central image of the west garden – an enormous coiled dragon rising from the sea, up through the storm clouds and into the heavens above.

The west garden constitutes the *hōjō*'s main garden at Ryōgin-an. It is a garden of contrasts: green-tinged *aoishi* represent the dragon's body heaving above the waves of the ocean (symbolised by white gravel of local Shirakawa granite) and swirling dark thunderclouds (represented by black gravel from

For the south *hōjō* garden at Ryōgin-an, Shigemori Mirei followed the ancient convention of having open ground leading from the gateway up to the *hōjō*. The bamboo fence is decorated with a design representing thunderbolts, in anticipation of the image of the dragon, the main motif of the adjacent west garden. Lightning also symbolises the flash of spiritual enlightenment.

OPPOSITE, LEFT and BELOW LEFT The west garden of the *hōjō* (abbot's hall) at Ryōgin-an represents a coiled dragon with a horned head. The white Shirakawa gravel symbolises the foaming sea and the black gravel, thunderclouds.

BELOW The east garden illustrates a legend associated with Ryōgin-an's founding abbot: as a child he was said to have been abandoned in the wilderness after succumbing to a high fever, but was protected from wolves by a pair of dogs. The stone in the centre represents the prone body of the sick child.

the upper reaches of the Ado River in Shiga prefecture). There are no plants in this garden – not even moss. The areas of white gravel are separated from the black by thin borders moulded from concrete.

Shigemori employed concrete in this way in other gardens, for example at Reiun-in, another sub-temple of Tōfuku-ji. Concrete allowed him to create shapes never before seen in Japanese gardens, and it had the added benefit, in Shigemori's view, of deterring the growth of moss. Shigemori had a profound understanding of the traditions of Japanese gardening, but, at the same time, he was keen to experiment with new materials and avant-garde designs.

According to the earliest surviving reference to the stone garden at Ryōan-ji, written in 1681, these stones were believed to symbolise tiger cubs crossing a river.

TORA-NO-KO-WATASHI: TIGER CUBS CROSSING A RIVER

In 1681, the physician Kurokawa Dōyū wrote in his book about his beloved adopted home Kyōto that the *kare-sansui* (dry-landscape) garden at Ryōan-ji was commonly believed to represent tiger cubs crossing a river. In this, Dōyū was referring to a Chinese fable about a tigress and her cubs. According to the legend, when a tigress gives birth to three cubs, one invariably turns out to be a leopard cub, which will devour its siblings if it is ever left alone with them. One day, a tigress comes to a river. She must ferry her cubs across it, but she can carry only one cub at a time, and she cannot leave her leopard cub alone with any of the others. So she first takes the leopard cub over and then goes back for one of the tiger cubs. When she has carried it over, she returns to her other tiger cub, taking her leopard cub back with her. She then leaves the leopard cub on the original bank and takes the second tiger cub across the river. Finally, she returns once more for the leopard cub, carries it across the river one last time, and the family is reunited.

Perhaps it was the presence of the one large boulder alongside the much smaller stones that made visitors to Ryōan-ji think of a family of tigers. Nonetheless, it is a mystery why the fable should have become associated with the Ryōan-ji garden, seeing that there are fifteen stones in it, not four. One theory is that, at the time Dōyū lived in Kyōto, the stone garden at Ryōan-ji was split into two sections by a roofed walkway, which extended from the gate in the south garden wall up to the *hōjō* (abbot's hall). If the stone representing the tigress was on one side of this walkway, and the 'cubs' on the other, the walkway itself could have stood for the river, especially if the structure had no walls and allowed a view of both gardens simultaneously. It is known, however, that, by 1791, the east side of the roofed walkway was certainly walled in, and, even if there was another garden on the other side, in no way could it have been considered a part of the main garden in front of the *hōjō*.

It is possible that Dōyū was not referring to the Chinese tiger fable at all, although the fable itself is an intriguing one that has inspired many Buddhist readings: for example, as an exhortation to persevere in the face of what seems to be an insurmountable difficulty; or as an illustration of the universality of Buddha's mercy, conveyed through the metaphor of the tigress's maternal solicitude that extended to both tiger and leopard cubs alike. Dōyū's contemporaries may have found the image of a family of tigers useful as a way of making sense of a garden design that did not feature familiar imagery such as a waterfall.

Another famous temple garden, which is popularly known as a *Tora-no-ko-watashi* (Tiger Cubs Crossing A River) garden is the south garden of the *dai-hōjō* (large hall), the larger of the two *hōjō* buildings, at Nanzen-ji. Tigers were a popular subject matter for ink-brush paintings (sometimes paired with dragons, since they were both associated with turbulent natural forces), and Nanzen-ji's smaller *hōjō* (*ko-hōjō*) possesses a particularly famous example of a set of *fusuma* (sliding partition-wall) paintings depicting tigers in a bamboo grove. This *ko-hōjō*, which is believed originally to have belonged either to Toyotomi Hideyoshi's Fushimi Castle or to have been a part of the Imperial Palace in Kyōto, was moved to its present location next to Nanzen-ji's *dai-hōjō* sometime between 1624 and 1644, during which time the *fusuma* paintings are thought to have been executed by the artist Kanō Tanyū. It is not known which was present there first – Tanyū's tiger paintings or the garden, which is generally attributed to Kobori Enshū and believed to have been constructed c.1630. Perhaps the garden inspired Tanyū's paintings, or the paintings could have encouraged admirers of Enshū's garden to call it by the same name as they had become accustomed to refer to the stone garden at Ryōan-ji.

Since the south garden of the *dai-hōjō* at Nanzen-ji is composed of six stones, it no more fits the Chinese tiger fable than the garden at Ryōan-ji, except that there is one stone on the far left that is noticeably larger than the other stones and anchors the entire composition. This garden is designed

LEFT and BELOW The *dai-hōjō* at Nanzen-ji, as seen from the corridor forming the east border of the south garden (left); this south garden of the *dai-hōjō* is popularly said to represent tiger cubs crossing a river, but Kobori Enshū employs forced perspective here in order to create the illusion of a landscape vanishing into the horizon (below).

OPPOSITE The dark grey stone, third from the right, symbolises Mikami-yama, known as the Mt Fuji of the land of Ōmi, from where Enshū's family originated.

to be viewed diagonally, and like the *kare-sansui* (dry-landscape) garden at Ryōan-ji it uses visual tricks to exaggerate the feeling of depth and distance. When seen from the east end of the *dai-hōjō*'s (large hall) veranda, the garden presents a receding vista. The six stones are set among moss and interplanted with trees along the south wall. They are in two staggered rows in decreasing order of size. Farther on, there are several even smaller azalea shrubs. Quite possibly, it was this feeling of progression that suggested the idea of a troupe of tigers slinking away into the distance.

As a variation on the theme of tiger cubs, the image of lion cubs has been traditionally applied to Shōden-ji's east garden, a marvellous dry garden that is perhaps unique in having no standing stones whatsoever. It has, instead, clipped mounds of mixed evergreen shrubs, with a magnificent distant view of Mt Hiei over the garden wall. The garden has long been considered another of Kobori Enshū's creations, although this attribution is now discounted. This association with Enshū is not altogether surprising when one considers that this ancient temple, originally founded in the thirteenth century, was revived towards the end of the sixteenth and the beginning of seventeenth

century through the efforts of, among others, Nanzen-ji's famous abbot Ishin Sūden, who commissioned Kobori Enshū to create Konchi-in's south garden. Shōden-ji's present *hōjō* (abbot's hall) was brought there from Konchi-in in 1652. But Enshū died in 1647, and it is highly unlikely that the garden was created before the installation of the *hōjō*.

The shrub-mounds in the garden at Shōden-ji resemble miniature tree-covered hillocks rising above a flat plain – or islands emerging from a sparkling ocean. When soft white clouds idyllically chase one another across a blue sky above Mt Hiei, the garden below seems like their reflection on the calm surface of a pond – the puffiness of the clouds being mirrored in the roundness of the shrubs. In total, there are fifteen of these mounds – the same as the number of stones in the garden at Ryōan-ji. But here they are loosely arranged into three large groups: from right to left, they consist of seven, five and three mounds. Just as in the south garden of the *dai-hōjō* at Nanzen-ji, there is a gradual but steady diminution of size from one side of the garden to the other. This gives a feeling of movement to the entire composition, as though a pride of lions were moving sedately across the brilliant white sands of a broad river.

SHŌDEN-JI

The Shōden-ji garden has the same minimalist feel as the garden at Ryōan-ji for a similar reason: an almost brutal restriction of materials to raked gravel and, in the case of Shōden-ji, evergreen shrubs. The geometry of the design, perhaps, is even more striking here, for the roundness of the shrubs and the gently sloping roof of the east gate of the garden make a vivid contrast to the straight horizontal lines formed by the rear garden wall and the stone blocks that edge the gravel garden. There is also a striking difference between the ordered formality within the walls of the garden and the soft luxuriance of the mixed woodland outside them. The temple is located on a steep hillside, and even higher slopes, covered with trees of towering growth, rise up on either side of it. (All of this land once belonged to Shōden-ji, but it was taken away from the temple by the Meiji government in 1871.) In the far distance rises the hazy blue outline of Mt Hiei. In autumn, the full moon can be seen, from the veranda of the *hōjō* (abbot's hall), rising to the right of Mt Hiei, travelling in an arc over the mountain and eventually sinking below the horizon to its left.

The east garden of Shōden-ji's *hōjō* has traditionally been said to symbolise lion cubs fording a river (below left); the garden's north gate, with a bowl in the foreground, to catch the run-off from the *hōjō's* roof (far left); a view of the east gate from a path that formerly led to the garden (centre left); flowering quince (*Chaenomeles speciosa*) is not native to Japan, but has been cultivated in the country since ancient times (left); a view towards Mt Hiei with the roof of Shōden-ji's *hōjō* in the foreground (below right).

The weighty pillars of Shinju-an's *hōjō* (abbot's hall) frame a view of the south garden.

SEVEN-FIVE-THREE GARDENS

The numbers seven, five and three are considered to be auspicious in Japan, and a combination of the three numerals is still often used as a theme on celebratory occasions. The most familiar of these is the *Shichi-go-san* (Seven-five-three) festival, which is held on 15 November, when boys of the age of three and five, and girls aged three and seven are taken to their local Shinto shrine. The origins of this festival go back to 1681. There are early seventeenth-century references to a type of celebratory banquet called the *shichi-go-san no furumai*, in which three trays of food were presented to each guest: the central tray would consist of seven separate dishes; the one to the right, five; and the one to the left, three. As the idea of *shichi-go-san* began to be incorporated into various social rituals, it started to make an appearance in the garden. The Shōden-ji temple garden, which has fifteen clipped mounds of evergreens divided into three groups of seven, five and three, respectively, was created sometime during the middle of the seventeenth century. Another temple with a garden strongly influenced by the *shichi-go-san* theme is Shinju-an, a sub-temple of Daitoku-ji.

Shinju-an is located next door to the sub-temple Daisen-in and on the north side of Daitoku-ji's *dai-hōjō* (large hall). Shinju-an had been on its current site for only about fourteen years when it burnt down, along with the rest of Daitoku-ji's large complex of buildings, in the Ōnin War. The famous Zen Buddhist monk Ikkyū Sōjun is said to have built a hermitage of sorts on the site of Shinju-an and stayed there during the 1470s, whenever he was in Kyōto in his capacity as Daitoku-ji's abbot. But Ikkyū's priority was rebuilding Daitoku-ji's main buildings, and Shinju-an itself was not properly rebuilt until 1491, a decade after Ikkyū's death. This was undertaken by one of Ikkyū's followers, the wealthy merchant Owa Sōrin, who had financed the reconstruction of Daitoku-ji's main *hōjō* (abbot's hall). The *hōjō* that Sōrin built for Shinju-an was, in turn, replaced with the present building in 1638.

This *hōjō* is a large imposing unadorned structure with wide verandas. Sombre and dignified, it stands in the south-east corner of the grounds of Shinju-an. The official approach to it is through a *genkan* (formal entrance) and porch, which forms the west side of the *hōjō*'s south garden. The path leading up to this gateway is designed with the seven-five-three numerical theme very much in mind. It uses stepping stones of widely differing shapes and sizes, and they are set out in sections that consist of seven, five and three stones, respectively. The pattern is rather like that of a hopscotch court. Oblong stones are used horizontally, as though to draw a line between groups of smaller stepping stones. Visual impact has been given priority over function, so that it is not always immediately obvious where one should place one's foot next. The gateway opens on to the *hōjō*'s main garden – the south garden – which is a rectangular space sparsely carpeted with moss and planted with a single pine tree, accompanied by five rounded, pincushion-shaped azaleas of differing sizes.

Around the east side of the *hōjō* there is a narrow moss garden tucked between the building and a pruned hedge of evergreens, which has an earthen wall and a copse of mature trees behind it. This garden features three groups of diminutive stones, which one might miss altogether if one were in a hurry and not paying careful attention to the surroundings. The point, of course, is not to hurry, but to take the opportunity to sit down – in the Japanese *seiza* (kneeling) position – on the veranda facing the garden. The veranda on this side of the *hōjō* is divided by *shōji* (sliding papered panels) into a wide interior veranda and a much narrower external one. When the *shōji* are drawn aside, they frame a view of the stones, which are arranged, from right to left, in groups of seven, five and three stones, respectively. Each of these groups is a mountain landscape in miniature. They are like *bonseki* (miniature landscapes mounted in pots), only here no containers are used. What is exquisite about the arrangements is the way in which the shapes and sizes of the stones are offset

RIGHT **The east garden** of Shinju-an's *hōjō* (abbot's hall) has three stone groupings: from right to left, they are made up of seven, five and three stones, respectively. The numbers are considered to be auspicious in Japan. The stones are intended to look as though they have been randomly placed, but, in fact, they balance each other beautifully in shape, size and colour.

OPPOSITE *Shōji* (sliding papered door panels) are drawn open to reveal a view of the middle group of stones. Each group can be appreciated as a self-contained composition.

against each other. After a summer thunderstorm, the wet stones glisten in the returning light, shadows exaggerating their craggy surfaces and turning creases and folds into deep crevices and steep-sided ravines. From the cool silent darkness of the veranda, the greenery of the moss, the low evergreen hedge and the tall trees look lush and refreshing.

Inevitably, there have been disagreements about when the east garden at Shinju-an was created. One opinion is that the stones are too small and too closely positioned to the *hōjō* (abbot's hall) to have originally been intended for the present building, and that, therefore, the garden must have been made for a smaller earlier building, which was a part of Sesshū's hermitage or part of the *hōjō* built by Owa Sōrin in 1491. Shigemori Mirei believed that

this garden must have been like the garden at Ryōan-ji, a stone garden laid with gravel and with no plants – certainly not the evergreen hedge, which now stands behind it. It is likely that it was once possible to see the city and Mt Hiei beyond the garden. But the trees have been allowed to grow tall, shutting out the modern world behind the illusion of a thick forest.

The east garden of the *hōjō* at Shūon-an has traditionally been said to symbolise the Sixteen *Rakan*, a group of Buddhist holy men. The stones are subtly positioned in such a way that they seem to be pointing towards the north-east corner of the garden, where there is a Shumisen arrangement, representing the mountain at the centre of the Buddhist cosmos.

THE SIXTEEN *RAKAN*

The east garden of the *dai-hōjō* (large hall) at Daitoku-ji is often described as a Garden of the Sixteen *Rakan*. The term *arakan*, or *rakan* for short, comes from the Sanskrit word *arhat*, denoting a holy man who has undergone spiritual training. In Chinese and Japanese Buddhism, there arose the tradition of venerating a group of sixteen *rakan*. Occasionally, two more were added, to make a total of eighteen. The *rakan* served as an exemplar of the religious way of life, and artistic representations of them in the form of statues and scroll paintings were frequently displayed at Zen Buddhist temples.

The east garden of the *dai-hōjō* at Daitoku-ji contains twenty stones altogether, rather than sixteen, so that calling it the Garden of the Sixteen *Rakan* is a general characterisation rather than a precise description. It is not known whether any reference to *rakan* was part of the intention of the original designer of the garden; perhaps, the idea of *rakan* was a convenient label by which later generations attempted to make sense of the garden. It is interesting that Shūon-an, which, like Daitoku-ji, has a very close association with the celebrated Zen Buddhist monk Ikkyū Sōjun, possesses a garden similar in style to the east garden of Daitoku-ji's *dai-hōjō*. Shūon-an's east garden, too, has traditionally been known as the Garden of the Sixteen *Rakan*.

Both the gardens at Daitoku-ji and at Shūon-an occupy a narrow space on the east side of the *hōjō* (abbot's hall) and serve as an adjunct to the south garden, which symbolises the sea. Unlike Daitoku-ji's *dai-hōjō*, however, Shūon-an has a north garden, which is connected to the south garden by the Garden of the Sixteen *Rakan*. This north garden is similar to the Daisen-in model: it faces the private, north-east room of the *hōjō* and consists of a cluster of fine stones representing a mountain landscape with a dry waterfall. There is, however, what looks like a flat *reihai-seki* (worship stone) in front of the massive boulder in the centre of the cluster, which suggests that the latter is intended to symbolise Shumisen. This would make the association of the stones in the east garden with Buddhist holy men very apt,

BELOW **The central stone** symbolises both Shumisen and Mt Hōrai at Shūon-an. Behind and slightly to the right of it are stones representing the head of a waterfall. An imaginary mountain stream winds its way around Shumisen in a series of tumbling cascades.

FOLLOWING PAGE Shūon-an's south *hōjō* garden symbolises the open sea. On the right is the *genkan* (formal entrance) with a porch leading up to the *hōjō*. The thatched roof belongs to Ikkyū's hermitage, the Kokyū-an, brought here from Kyōto in 1467. Ikkyū's mausoleum is on its left.

especially since the largest of these stones has a marked slant that makes it appear as though it is facing in the direction of the Shumisen stone.

As in the case with the garden at Daisen-in, the symbolic river at Shūon-an cascading down the dry waterfall divides, as it were, with one branch proceeding along the north side of the *hōjō* (abbot's hall), past a stone-and-azalea arrangement representing a combined turtle-and-crane island. This indicates that the Shumisen stone doubles for Mt Hōrai. The other branch of the imaginary river runs southwards along the east garden – the Garden of the Sixteen *Rakan*

– towards the south garden of the *hōjō*, with its open expanse of sparkling white gravel symbolising the sea. The Garden of the Sixteen *Rakan* is a cheerful space with the stones set in moss among tiny Satsuki azaleas, ferns and *Ardisia crenata*. Tall Japanese black pines (*Pinus thunbergii*) have been planted among them at regular intervals. A garden wall runs along the back of this garden, yet it is not an oppressive presence – its warm tone adding brightness to the scene.

While the Garden of the Sixteen *Rakan* suggests a mountain ravine, the south garden represents a vast seascape. The bank to the rear of this garden

is planted with pruned azaleas, as if to suggest islands in the far horizon. The addition of exotic sago palms (*Cycas revoluta*), with their flaring leaves, imparts a tropical feel to the garden, as though one were looking out on to a southern ocean. This is the garden that faces the public rooms of the *hōjō*: its all-embracing tranquillity suggests the state of spiritual calm that the great Ikkyū Sōjun himself finally attained at the end of his long and eventful life.

According to temple tradition, these gardens surrounding the *hōjō* were designed collaboratively by the calligrapher, artist and tea master Shōkadō

Shōjō, the poet Sakawada Masatoshi (or Shōshun, also known as Sakawada Kiroku) and the poet and scholar of Confucianism Ishikawa Jōzan. Jōzan's former house in Kyōto, along with its superb garden, became the Shisen-dō, a Zen Buddhist temple of the Sōtō school, in 1966.

But there is a difficulty with this legend. Shūon-an's present *hōjō* is not contemporaneous with Ikkyū, but was donated by the *daimyō* (feudal lord) Maeda Toshitsune, when he undertook the restoration of the temple in 1650. Shōjō, however, died in 1639 and Kiroku in 1643.

This minute courtyard garden is located between Ryōgen-in's *kuri* (domestic quarters) and its *hōjō* (abbot's hall): the pair of rocks at the south end of the garden resemble mountains out of a Chinese ink-brush painting (left); the garden seen from the corridor leading from the *kuri* to the *hōjō* (centre); a view of the garden towards the corridor, where in ancient times tea was prepared for guests attending temple ceremonies, and, beyond it, is a well and the end section of a long garden facing the temple's *shoin* (reception hall) (right).

THE TŌTEKIKO GARDEN AT RYŌGEN-IN

Nabeshima Gakushō worked with Shigemori Mirei surveying historic gardens across Japan in the 1930s. This exquisite courtyard garden, named the Tōtekiko (Courtyard of a Drop of East Water), is probably his best-known work and his masterpiece. Occupying a tiny space between the *hōjō* (abbot's hall) and the *kuri* (domestic quarters), it is one of the smallest *kare-sansui* (dry-landscape) gardens in Japan. The name of the garden suggests the idea that each droplet of water trickling off a mountainside will eventually become part of the mighty ocean. The concentric circles around the stones are reminiscent of the ripples that are formed when a rock is cast into water or a frog jumps into a pond. They are a reminder of the repercussions of the smallest of events.

THE OX

In the garden at Daisen-in, there is a large unwieldy stone said to look like a reclining ox raising its head. Another ox-shaped stone can be seen in the moss garden of the seventeenth-century Zen Buddhist temple Enkō-ji in Kyōto, where it stands among Japanese maples and Satsuki azaleas.

The image of the ox derives from the artistic convention of the Ten Ox-herding Pictures, which represent the ten stages involved in the attainment of enlightenment. The best-known series is the one attributed to the twelfth- to thirteenth-century Chinese Chán monk Kuòān Shīyuǎn (Kakuan Shion in Japanese). The first seven pictures consist of (1) a boy searching for a lost ox; (2) the boy discovering the ox's hoof prints; (3) the boy spotting the ox hiding behind a tree; (4) the boy attempting to capture the recalcitrant ox; (5) the boy taming the ox; (6) the boy riding home on the ox's back, playing his flute; (7) the boy reaching home and forgetting all about the ox. The eighth picture is left blank. The ninth depicts natural scenery, and the last shows the boy, who has become a monk, setting out for town.

The ox in the series symbolises the true self. Taming the self – that is, becoming enlightened to Buddhist truths – is shown as only an intermediate stage. True enlightenment involves forgetting the ox – the self – altogether. The sequence ends with the reminder that the Buddhist monk must not sit alone in his enlightened solitude, but go back among the people to assist them in their struggles towards enlightenment.

The north garden of the *hōjō* at Zuihō-in was designed by Shigemori Mirei in honour of the *daimyō* (feudal lord) Ōtomo Sōrin, who founded this Daitoku-ji sub-temple before his conversion to Christianity. The seven stones form the shape of a cross when viewed from one particular direction.

ZUIHŌ-IN AND THE IMAGE OF THE CROSS

The Daitoku-ji sub-temple Zuihō-in is said to have been founded by Ōtomo Yoshishige, known as Ōtomo Sōrin, a powerful sixteenth-century *daimyō* (feudal lord) who is famous for having converted to Catholicism. Born in the modern-day prefecture of Ōita in the north-east region of the island of Kyūshū, he was initially an ardent follower of Zen Buddhism — as were most of his family. In 1562, he took the first steps towards entering the Buddhist priesthood, adopting the name Sōrin. But as an important local ruler on the island of Kyūshū, he had met the Jesuit missionary Francis Xavier back in 1551. Sōrin was a highly cultured man, and he enthusiastically promoted trade with the Portuguese. He also extended his protection to Catholic missionaries. Gradually, he became attracted to Christianity, and after a great deal of vacillation between the two religions, he was baptised in 1578.

When the garden historian and designer Shigemori Mirei was commissioned in 1961 to create gardens for Zuihō-in's *hōjō* (abbot's hall), he decided that one of them should pay tribute to Sōrin's Christian faith. At first glance, the north garden of the *hōjō* looks like a traditional *kare-sansui* (dry-landscape)

garden. White gravel is used to symbolise the sea, moss to indicate dry land, and seven stones to represent islands and mountains. The gravel is raked in deep diagonal lines, suggesting regular rolling waves. A prominent stone has been placed on the edge of the moss in the familiar way stones have been employed for centuries in Japanese gardens, to designate a shoreline. This stone, however, serves as a pivot for the entire design of the garden, for the seven standing stones resolve themselves into the form of a cross — with this particular stone at its centre — when they are viewed from the north-east corner of the *hōjō*'s veranda.

The imaginary vertical axis of the cross extends all the way to the tiny courtyard garden, which flanks the east side of the *hōjō*. This line terminates in a stone lantern with two short round protruding arms — a type of stone lantern known as an *Oribe-tōrō*, because it was a style favoured by the influential tea master Furuta Oribe. This type of lantern has a thick shaft, which was frequently carved with a standing figure, usually representing a Buddhist bodhisattva. After Christianity came to be proscribed in Japan in the seventeenth century, Christians were said to have kept lanterns of this shape because their

BELOW LEFT The small courtyard garden between Zuihō-in's *hōjō* and *kuri* (domestic quarters) features a lantern in a style closely associated with the early Christian community in Japan. The garden is planted with hedge bamboos and balloon flowers (*Platycodon grandiflorus*).

OPPOSITE BELOW Zuihō-in's south *hōjō* garden symbolises Mt Hōrai, as well as the mountain retreat of a great Chinese Chán (Zen) master. There is an allusion to Jesus's Sermon on the Mount. Shigemori Mirei also manages to incorporate the image of the dragon.

OPPOSITE LEFT The pattern in the gravel is 10 cm/4 inches deep, and it takes the abbot, Maeda Shōdō, forty minutes to rake this garden alone, which he does weekly as well as after heavy rainstorms.

OPPOSITE CENTRE: Beyond the south garden is a tea garden: the two are separated by a shallow stone bridge spanning the gravel.

OPPOSITE RIGHT These stepping stones lead from the *hōjō* through the tea garden to the Yokei-an tea room.

protruding arms made them look vaguely cross-like. Their lanterns were, moreover, reputed to be carved with a figure that stood for the Virgin or a Christian saint, but that could be explained to suspicious government officials as being a representation of a bodhisattva. It is not known how old the lantern at Zuihō-in is, and its shank is sunk deep in the ground so that the carved figure (if there is one) is invisible.

The north garden of the *hōjō* (abbot's hall) is popularly known as the Garden of the Cross, but it has the formal name Kanmin-tei (Garden of Quiet Sleep), taken from a Zen Buddhist metaphor for spiritual peace. This garden's theme of hard-won tranquillity is overlaid with the story of one man's search for religious truth. It also serves as a reminder of the early history of Christianity in Japan. The north garden shares its theme with the south *hōjō* garden, which also represents the struggles of a religious man – this time a Zen master. Here, a curved row of rugged stones emerges out of the gravel garden like a chain of mountain islands rising out of the sea. The gravel is raked in a pattern of concentric circles, which convey the impression of fierce waves pounding on the desolate shores of the stark rocky islands. This garden gets its name – Dokuza-tei (Garden of Solitary Meditation) – from a saying attributed to the eighth- to ninth-century Chinese Chán master Bǎizhàng Huáihái (known as Hyakujō Ekai in Japan): 'I sit (meditating) in solitude on the Great Sublime Peak.' Bǎizhàng founded a Chán Buddhist temple on Mt Bǎizhàng, from which he got his nickname; the mountain is in the province of Jiāngxī and had the alternative name Dàxióng-fēng (Great Sublime Peak). Hence, the garden is a symbolic representation of Bǎizhàng's own heroic struggle towards enlightenment. It also symbolises the great Zen master's enlightened state – man becomes one with the mountain and with the entire universe.

For many decades, if not centuries, the *shakkei* was lost here at Entsū-ji. Eventually, in 1955, the decision was made – under the guidance of the garden historian and architect Nakane Kinsaku – to cut down most of the trees and shrubs that had grown up in and around the garden.

THE BORROWED LANDSCAPE

Entsū-ji is one of the best-known examples of a Japanese garden with a *shakkei* (borrowed landscape). Its *kyaku-den* (guest hall) faces eastwards on to a flat, *kare-sansui* (dry-landscape), moss garden bordered by an evergreen hedge and a row of conifers, between the trunks of which there soars a magnificent view of Mt Hiei.

This garden was founded on the site of Hata'eda Palace, a villa built by the seventeenth-century emperor Go-Mizuno'o among the hills to the north of Kyōto. Go-Mizuno'o was a prolific builder of villas and gardens, and he restlessly sought out locations with the best scenic views, where he might, finally, be able to realise his perfect retreat. Go-Mizuno'o's reign was marked by a bitter power struggle with the Tokugawa shogunate. He abdicated in 1629, but continued to rule over the imperial court until his death in 1680. Four of his children became emperors during his lifetime, the last of whom survived him.

Several famous Kyōto gardens are associated with Go-Mizuno'o. The Ninomaru Garden at Nijō Castle in Kyōto was extensively remodelled by Kobori Enshū in preparation for a visit from the emperor in 1626. Go-Mizuno'o himself designed the layout of Shūgaku-in Rikyū, his most famous villa, with its distinguished garden built among the south-west foothills of Mt Hiei.

During the 1640s, Go-Mizuno'o's attention was focused on the scenic foothills of north Kyōto, where he built a clutch of villas, including Hata'eda Palace. Once he had begun work on Shūgaku-in Rikyū, *c.*1655, he lost interest in these other villas. Hata'eda Palace was eventually given to a nun, a noblewoman who had once been the wet nurse to Go-Mizuno'o's son, the emperor Reigen. In 1678, she founded a Zen Buddhist temple there, and a building from the palace belonging to Go-Mizuno'o's empress was brought to serve as its *kyaku-den* (guest hall). It is not known whether the temple's famous *kare-sansui* garden was built while the place was still an imperial villa

or after it had become a temple, but it is in a style that has much in common with Zen temple gardens of the early seventeenth century.

A rectangular garden extends the whole length of the east façade of the *kyaku-den* (guest hall) at Entsū-ji. Instead of having garden walls, the garden is enclosed by a trimmed evergreen hedge, which includes evergreen oaks and camellias. On the far right-hand side of the garden, alongside the veranda, there is a large clipped azalea. This is balanced by the arrangement of stones set among the moss towards the left side of the garden. Straight ahead between the two is the view of Mt Hiei. Instead of having a *tsukiyama* (man-made hillock) in the fashion of many traditional Japanese gardens, the Entsū-ji garden audaciously incorporates Mt Hiei itself into its design.

The garden stones include not only expensive *aoishi* (chlorite schist) from present-day Wakayama, but also ochre-coloured, local mountain stone and some banded stones from the coast. Despite the variety of colour and patterning, most of the stones are buried very deeply so that relatively little protrudes above ground. None of the stones is allowed to compete with the height of the hedge. They are arranged broadly in three sweeping arcs,

which fill the left-hand side of the garden. Although there are more than forty in number, the stones look neither cramped nor jumbled. Their effect is to accentuate the openness of the rest of the garden. The garden is now carpeted in moss, but, originally, it is likely to have been a gravel garden, with moss, if any, only immediately around the stones.

The elegant restraint with which the stones are employed in the Entsū-ji garden is comparable to the understated sophistication of the garden at the Myōshin-ji sub-temple Zakke-in, which has been attributed to the Nichiren Buddhist monk Gyokuen. Just as in that garden, clipped azaleas of differing heights are used in the Entsu-ji garden to soften the severity of the stones. Because of the similarity in style between the two gardens, there has been some speculation that the one at Entsū-ji might also have been by Gyokuen, who died in 1661. Whether or not this is correct, this garden was certainly executed by somebody with an exquisite eye for compositional harmony.

The garden at Entsu-ji is one of the largest rectangular gardens in the whole of Kyōto. The evergreen hedge is 1.6 m/5¼ ft tall. Yet, when viewed from the *kyaku-den*, it does not give the impression of being particularly high. The hedge

OPPOSITE Views of distant mountains have been incorporated into the composition of these paintings of Chinese landscapes by the sixteenth- to seventeenth-century Japanese artist Kanō Sanraku. These *fusuma* (sliding partition walls) form part of the *danna-no-ma* (reception room) of Shōden-ji's *hōjō* (abbot's hall).

BELOW The layout of stones in the Entsū-ji garden bears a similarity to the design of the south *hōjō* garden at Zakke-in, seen here in an illustration from the 1799 guidebook *Miyako Rinsen Meishō Zue*.

The gravel and shrubs in the foreground, the trees beyond the wall and the woodland in the middle distance, together with the distant view of Mt Hiei and the clouds in the sky, all come together to create a feeling of great depth. The middle group of shrubs is modelled loosely on a *sanzon-seki* (three sacred stones) arrangement, with a shrub representing a *reihai-seki* (worship stone) in front. The trees beyond the wall require careful maintenance in order to preserve the borrowed vista. Lightning strikes on the tall trees are also a constant danger.

does, however, split the field of vision horizontally into half. Above it looms the hazy outline of Mt Hiei. Below it is the velvety green, enclosed garden, with the azalea by the veranda in the foreground and the garden stones occupying the middle ground. There is a strong sense of the near distance, the middle distance and the far distance: this is accentuated by the pillars of the *kyaku-den* and, farther off, by the row of *Cryptomeria japonica* and *Chamaecyparis obtusa* along the hedge. These tall trees, which have had their side branches trimmed off, add crisp vertical lines to the composition of the garden, intersecting with the straight horizontal line of the hedge. They have the effect of 'framing' the view of Mt Hiei. Thus, through the use of forced perspective, the scale of the garden and the view of Mt Hiei are beautifully balanced.

The combination of near, middle and far distance was an important element in the composition of Chinese ink brush landscape paintings, and it was something Japanese garden designers picked up from the traditions of Chinese art. The appearance of Mt Hiei changes with every flickering play of light on the gossamer haze, which descends and lifts from the face of the mountain through the course of the day and through the seasons. A ray of brilliant sunshine will pick out individual details of the mountainside with great clarity, while in the soft spring sunshine the mountain is bathed in a bluish grey wash, which makes it look distant and ethereal.

This effect is even more pronounced at Shōden-ji, where a view of Mt Hiei constitutes a *shakkei* (borrowed landscape) for its *hōjō* (abbot's hall) garden. Shōden-ji is located farther west than Entsū-ji, and Mt Hiei looks much smaller and less imposing from here. However, Shōden-ji is set on a much steeper, more heavily wooded hillside, and the contrast between the brilliant sparkling whiteness of the gravel of the walled garden in the foreground, the deep pine green of the trees beyond the garden wall, and the smoky outline of Mt Hiei against the sky makes the composition seem even more like a Chinese ink-brush painting than the garden at Entsū-ji.

ZEN TEMPLE GARDENS AND THE TEA GARDEN

The connection between tea and Buddhist temples is an ancient one. It is not known when tea drinking was first introduced into Japan from China, but the earliest historical references to the custom date back to the second decade of the ninth century, by which time tea was already being served at Buddhist temples. But the custom failed to take firm hold, and it was revived only after the monk Myōan Yōsai brought the seeds of the tea plant, along with the tenets of Zen Buddhism, back with him from China in the latter half of the twelfth century. Yōsai was a firm believer in the medicinal benefits of tea drinking. He was convinced it strengthened the powers of the body, mind and soul. The practice of drinking tea became firmly established at Zen Buddhist temples, being drunk both on formal occasions by the assembled temple community, and individually by monks who found it helped to dispel drowsiness during meditation.

The cultivation of tea plants gradually spread outside the confines of Buddhist temples, and a taste for the beverage began to percolate through the Japanese population. Among the cultured aristocracy and high-ranking bushi (members of the military class), the fashion for tea drinking became intertwined with their fascination with Chinese fine and decorative arts. Chinese tea ware and utensils were highly sought after. Then came an architectural innovation: the shoin (private study). By the fifteenth century, the shoin provided the ideal intimate space both for displaying prized collectibles and entertaining guests. Such rooms were designed so that a section of the tatami matting could be removed, revealing a hearth that was useful not only for providing warmth but also for heating water during the preparation of tea. One of the earliest examples of a shoin can be seen in the Tōgu-dō building at Ginkaku-ji, the Temple of the Silver Pavilion.

The serving and drinking of tea became an occasion for admiring exquisite Chinese wares in the elegant surroundings of a shoin. It involved the cultivation of a discerning taste for all that was refined and graceful. On one occasion in the 1580s, Sen no Rikyū prepared and served tea to Toyotomi Hideyoshi in the beautiful shoin, which is part of the hōjō (abbot's hall) at the Daitoku-ji

sub-temple Daisen-in. This room looks out on to Daisen-in's lavish *kare-sansui* (dry-landscape) garden. Hideyoshi demanded to know where Rikyū was going to put his tea-room flower arrangement. By way of a reply, the tea master is said to have poured water from a flower vase over the magnificent, smooth-topped, purple-tinged stone that is positioned next to the veranda and placed a single flower stalk on its glistening surface.

Rikyū is famous for having perfected an altogether different style of tea ceremony, known as *wabi-cha*, which emphasised simplicity rather than the connoisseurship of fine Chinese antiques. The first steps towards the formation of this new aesthetic were taken by the fifteenth-century Buddhist monk and tea master Murata Jukō, of whom it is related that he preferred to take tea in the simple surroundings of a thatched cottage with a single ink-brush painting for decoration. Outside the cottage, he laid out stones so that they resembled a view of faraway mountains. Jukō was described as having a taste for what was *ko'tan* (old and faded). But his approach was neither a high-handed nor a naive rejection of the *shoin* (private study) style of presenting tea. Far from

it – he made the study of Chinese art a prerequisite for his own style of tea. Jukō disapproved of cultural arrogance, but neither did he condone ignorance.

The sixteenth-century tea master Takeno Jō'ō was the first to apply the idea of *wabi* (from the verb *wabu*, meaning 'to enjoy tranquillity') to the *ko'tan* tastes of Jukō. For Jō'ō, an important aspect of *wabi* was unpretentiousness. He associated *wabi* with autumn rain and the autumn of life – with the acceptance of age, of change, of solitude, of death. Jō'ō is said to have remarked that it is only by experiencing the beauty of the cherry blossoms in spring and the glorious colours of the maple leaves in autumn that one comes to a full appreciation of the quiet solitude of the humble thatched cottage. It was Jō'ō who popularised *wabi-cha*. In his eyes, the tea ceremony was all about hospitality: the host extended a courteous welcome to his guests, who reciprocated with their sincere, whole-hearted appreciation of the hospitality that was being offered to them. This struck a cord among his followers, many of whom were high-ranking *bushi* (members of the military class). Jō'ō was himself descended from a samurai family, although his orphaned father had

The east veranda of the *shoin* (reception hall) at Jikō-in serves as a *machi-ai* (tea-garden bench) from which stepping stones lead to the entrance of the inner *roji* (tea garden) of the Kōrin-an tea room (right); the path through the inner *roji* leads to a stone basin for cleansing the mouth and hands (far right); the entrance to the Kōrin-an is in the form of a *nijiri-guchi* (square entrance), and the tea room must be entered on one's knees (below far right); the stepping stones continue around the tea room to a second garden gate (below right).

settled in the port city of Sakai. Jō'ō had disciples who belonged to that city's affluent merchant community, and among that group was Sen no Rikyū.

Sen no Rikyū formalised the tea ceremony. He laid out precepts for how he believed the ceremony should be organised and conducted. He did not advocate rules for the sake of having rules, but to make true freedom possible. Freedom was not to be mistaken for an absence of order or a lack of technique. Only the mastery of the fundamental rules could open the way for real individuality; otherwise, there was only chaos.

Rikyū's approach was reflected in the design of his tea rooms and of the gardens that surrounded them. In Jō'ō's day, tea rooms each had a veranda and were entered through *shōji* (conventional sliding door panels pasted with translucent rice paper). The only light to enter the tea room was through the *shōji*. This suited Jō'ō, who felt that strong sunlight was anathema for the proper appreciation of tea utensils. He preferred the entrance to a tea room to face north, but he did not want its front garden to be planted with shrubs or trees lest they obstructed the tea room's one source of light. Nor did he approve of other kinds of traditional garden ornament – handsome garden stones, pretty pebbles or glittering white gravel – because he felt they would distract the attention of those participating in the tea ceremony. Jō'ō's type of tea garden – in fact, no more than a tiny rectangular open yard – was known as a *tsubo-no-uchi*. The term was also applied to the narrow passage or side 'garden' by which some of these tea rooms were accessed.

Sen no Rikyū did away with the veranda and the *shōji*, and created the *nijiri-guchi* (a small square entranceway through which one has to pass in a kneeling position). Instead of having all the light enter the tea room through the *nijiri-guchi*, Rikyū added windows, which allowed diffused light to filter into the room from several directions. He preferred to have his tea rooms face south, but he planted evergreen trees and shrubs in the garden to block direct sunlight. He liked the way tall branches broke up a view: he is said to have found the moon much more interesting and affecting when glimpsed from between the branches of a tree or through strands of cloud.

The evolution of the *chaniwa* or *chatei* (Japanese tea garden) is inseparable from the history of the cultural discipline *chadō* or *sadō* (the formal tea ceremony). For Rikyū, the tea ceremony was more than just the preparation and drinking of a beverage. The act of hospitality began the moment the guests arrived at the outer gate. The garden through which they passed in order to reach the tea room played an essential role in getting the guests into the proper frame of mind for the tea ceremony. The tea garden eased the transition from the hurly-burly of everyday life to the tranquil intimacy of the tea room. Rikyū wanted his trees and shrubs to create the feeling of a country retreat, and, to that end, he insisted that they should not be heavily pruned, but left to form their own natural shapes. He used stepping stones not only for their rustic appearance but also to encourage guests to walk more slowly through the garden.

Rikyū was one of the first to employ stone lanterns in the garden. Until then, they had been predominantly votive objects erected within the grounds of Buddhist temples and Shinto shrines. Just as water basins are provided at Shinto shrines so that worshippers can purify themselves before prayer, Rikyū placed stone basins alongside his garden path, so that guests could cleanse themselves before the tea ceremony by washing their hands and rinsing their mouths. Every stage of the tea ceremony, however tiny, emphasised the importance of the here and now.

The tea ceremony is certainly not a religious ritual, Zen or otherwise. However, certain aspects of *wabi-cha* (rustic style of tea ceremony) – its emphasis on simplicity, purity, sincerity and calmness – were strongly influenced by Zen Buddhist meditation practices. Murata Jukō, Takeno Jō'ō and Sen no Rikyū were all adherents of Zen Buddhism: Jukō entered a Buddhist temple as a novice at the age of ten, and later in life studied Zen Buddhism under the famous

BELOW Stepping stones lead up to the *nijiri-guchi* (square entrance) to a teahouse in the grounds of Kōrin-in, a Daitoku-ji sub-temple. This teahouse is in a style favoured by the tea master Furuta Oribe and has a conventionally sized entrance for high-ranking guests, as well as a low *nijiri-guchi*. Kōrin-in also possesses a *hōjō* (abbot's hall) garden in the *kare-sansui* (dry-landscape) style, which has been restored by Nakane Kinsaku.

OPPOSITE An autumnal flower arrangement in a standing stone basin at Kōrin-in.

Ikkyū Sōjun. Like Jō'ō before him, Rikyū practised meditation at Nanshū-ji — a Rinzai Zen Buddhist temple in the city of Sakai with strong links to Daitoku-ji, the great Kyōto temple with which he later became closely associated. Rikyū's grandson Sōtan was sent to Daitoku-ji as a young boy, and he is said to have drawn strongly on his religious training once he became a tea master. Three of his own sons founded the three main schools of tea in existence today — the Omote Sen-ke, the Ura Sen-ke and the Musha-no-kōji Sen-ke.

By the late seventeenth century, there was a movement to reinterpret and consolidate Rikyū's teachings in the light of Zen Buddhism. A famous treatise on tea, entitled the *Nampō-roku*, characterises the tea ceremony as a quasi-religious ritual, and connects the idea of *wabi* (the aesthetic appreciation of tranquillity) to Buddhist piety, the seeking of purity, and the simplicity of the Zen Buddhist way of life. Rikyū's type of tea garden, the *roji*, was originally written with Chinese characters signifying a path, but it then began to be written with the Chinese characters meaning 'dewy ground' (but still pronounced *roji*). 'Dewy ground' is a Buddhist term used in the *Lotus Sutra* as a metaphor for a state of being, in which one is free from all passions and desires, sorrow and pain.

This swing back towards simplicity was largely a reaction to the way in which the tea ceremony developed after Rikyū's death. Notwithstanding Rikyū's own advocacy of simplicity, his main patrons were the most powerful men in the country — the warlord Oda Nobunaga and, after his death, Toyotomi Hideyoshi. Most of Rikyū's closest disciples were also military commanders and *daimyō* (feudal lords), such as Furuta Oribe and Hosokawa Sansai. Oribe, for one, was very conscious of his social status, and he was uncomfortable following Rikyū's example of treating everybody in the tea room as equals, regardless of their actual rank. Oribe also considered Rikyū's style to be too austere and self-effacing.

Oribe had a brilliant eye for innovative design, and, quite contrary to Rikyū's view that nothing about the tea ceremony should be obtrusive, he enjoyed producing striking, if not shocking, visual effects. He is best remembered now for his predilection for extreme asymmetry in ceramics – lopsided tea bowls and squashed-in vases, for example. But Oribe also created vivid visual contrasts in his tea gardens. Contemporary accounts relate how, in one garden, he juxtaposed a section containing only black, wave-smoothed beach stones as ground cover with another in which he laid out perfectly aligned, dry pine needles.

Whereas Rikyū sought to recreate as naturalistic a setting as possible in his *roji* (tea gardens), Oribe deliberately drew attention to the artifice. He used pine needles under trees that were not pines, and even installed dead trees in some of his gardens. Rikyū appreciated the accidental: he told his disciples to sweep the *roji* clean several hours before the arrival of the guests, but not to touch any leaves that fell subsequently. Oribe, on the other hand, instructed his disciples to scatter leaves around the *roji* after they had tidied it up. For Rikyū, the main purpose of stepping stones was to provide a path: he wanted them to look as though they were something one might come across on a mountainside, but he also wished them to be comfortable to walk on. For Oribe – and for his main disciple Kobori Enshū – paths became an opportunity to experiment with elaborate patterns, which combined stones of different shapes and colours, both naturally shaped and cut.

Into the *roji* Oribe introduced *sute-ishi* (single stones that were there only because they were beautiful and served no other purpose other than to be ornamental). In this way, the *roji* came more and more to resemble a decorative *shoin* (reception hall) garden, meant to be appreciated from indoors. While Oribe, like Rikyū, strictly forbade trees in the *roji* to be deliberately pruned into a contrived shape (although, unlike his master, he approved of trees that had naturally grown into an arresting form), Kobori Enshū did not feel that trees in the *roji* should be treated any differently from trees in a *shoin* garden. By his day, the distinction between the *roji* and the *shoin* garden was no longer being made.

KŌTŌ-IN

This sub-temple, which belongs to Daitoku-ji, is famous for its glorious Japanese maples. It was founded by the *daimyō* (feudal lord) Hosokawa Tadaoki (also known as Hosokawa Sansai) in 1601. Sansai was a poet, a military leader and a distinguished tea master. Along with Furuta Oribe, he was one of Sen no Rikyū's closest disciples.

At Kōtō-in, Japanese maples line the long straight paved avenue, which leads from the outer gate to the *genkan* (formal entrance). The *genkan* opens on to the south garden of the *hon-dō* (sanctuary), which is also referred to as the *kyaku-den* (guest hall). This south garden is simplicity itself, being a moss-covered, rectangular space planted with Japanese maples and enclosed by thickets of bamboo. It features a single large stone lantern, a quiet memorial to the turbulent lives of members of the Hosokawa family.

This lantern is a copy of a famous original, which was bequeathed to Hosokawa Sansai by his tea master Sen no Rikyū in 1591. The original lantern now stands over the grave of Sansai and his wife in another part of the grounds of Kōtō-in. It was much admired in its day, and was coveted by Rikyū's master Toyotomi Hideyoshi. In order not to have to give it to him, Rikyū is supposed to have smashed a portion of the back of the lantern cage. Sansui, who like his associate Furuta Oribe

OPPOSITE The path leading from Kōtō-in's outer gateway to its inner *genkan* (formal entrance) is very simple and is designed in geometrical lines. Its style is in sharp contrast to the rustic stepping stones encountered later in Kōtō-in's tea garden.

BELOW The single stone lantern in the beautiful south garden of Kōtō-in's *hon-dō* (sanctuary) is a simple, yet moving tribute to the members of the Hosokawa clan, whose ashes are buried at this temple.

LEFT This stone basin is traditionally described as being in the shape of a *kesa* (Buddhist monk's surplice), but it is likely to have originally been a foundation stone of an imperial gate in the Korean capital Hanseong.

BELOW The rustic bamboo gate here leads into the inner *roji* (tea garden) of the Shōkō-ken tea room.

had a strong taste for asymmetry, is believed later to have broken part of the roof over the lantern cage and the side of one of the windows.

The area to the west of the *hon-dō* (sanctuary) at Kōtō-in is thickly planted with mature trees to create the impression of woodland. It is criss-crossed with stepping stone paths, and in one part there is a dell in which a monumental stone basin has been set. This behemoth is thought to have originally been a foundation stone of a gateway to the Korean royal palace in Hanseong (modern-day Seoul), brought back by the warlord Katō Kiyomasa after the two Japanese invasions of Korea in 1592–3 and 1597–8. This basin was a favourite of Sansai's, as was the stone lantern bequeathed to him by Rikyū, and wherever he travelled in Japan he took both of these massive pieces of stonework with him.

The stepping stones serve as paths leading to the temple's two tea rooms. On the day of a tea ceremony, the host chooses which path his guests should

BELOW **These tiny tea gardens** are artfully designed to create
the illusion that the guest is walking through a wooded rural
landscape (left); bamboos and evergreens in the outer *roji* of the Shōkō-
ken tea room provide a striking foil for the brilliant autumn colours of
the maples (centre); stepping stones lead through the inner *roji* (tea
garden) past an *Enkianthus perulatus* in flaming autumn colour (right).

BELOW FAR RIGHT **A stone tied** with black hemp-palm rope is used
in tea gardens to indicate to guests which stepping stones should
not be followed.

take to reach a particular tea room, and directs them by placing stones tied with black hemp-palm rope on the stepping stones that they should not use.

The way in which the trees and shrubs have been planted and maintained at Kōtō-in reflects the naturalistic style of *roji* (tea garden) beloved by Hosokawa Sansai's tea master Sen no Rikyū. One of the tea rooms is actually part of the principal room of the *hon-dō* (sanctuary). But it can be screened off (if so desired) from the rest of the room with the insertion of *fusuma* (sliding partition walls), and it has its own *nijiri-guchi* (square entrance) from the garden outside. The other tea room – the Shōkō-ken – is in a rustic hermitage style, and its design is believed to be one that was favoured by Hosokawa Sansai. This tea room has an inner *roji*, which is separated from the rest of the temple garden by a low bamboo gate.

Sansai founded Kōtō-in in honour of his father, Hosokawa Fujitaka (known as Hosokawa Yūsai), who himself had refounded Daishin-in sub-temple at Myōshi-ji and, in 1602, had assisted in the restoration of Tenju-an sub-temple at Nanzen-ji. Sansai invited the abbot of Daitoku-ji, Gyokuho Jōsō – who also happened to be his father's younger half-brother – to become Kōtō-in's first abbot. The brothers had been born into the Mitsubuchi clan, and it was during Gyokuho Jōsō's tenure as abbot of Daitoku-ji that Daisen-in's famous garden stones were possibly moved there from the Mitsubuchi family residence.

RIGHT There is a bench along this corridor between Shinju-an's *hōjō* and the *shoin* (reception hall) building called the Tsūsen-in; it serves as a *machi-ai* (tea garden bench) and there are steps in front of it leading to a stone basin.

OPPOSITE A garden wall with a gate separates the *hōjō*'s east garden (which doubles as the outer tea garden for the Tei'gyoku-ken tea room) from the Tsūsen-in garden (which serves as the middle tea garden) (top); the Tei'gyoku-ken tea room is next to the north-east corner of the Tsūsen-in (bottom).

SHINJU-AN

The Daitoku-ji sub-temple Shinju-an is famous for its Shichi-go-san Garden, located on the east side of its imposing *hōjō* (abbot's hall). What is not immediately obvious when viewing this garden is that it actually serves as part of an outer *roji* (tea garden). It is different from a traditional *roji* in that it is intended to be seen from the veranda, not by walking through it. But, farther along the veranda, it is possible to step down on to a path of stepping stones leading to a gate in the garden wall, which runs along the north side of the *hōjō*. This gate opens on to the middle *roji*.

The middle *roji* at Shinju-an faces a hall called the Tsūsen-in. This building was originally the dressing hall of a wife of the emperor Ōgimachi. It was given to a physician in gratitude for a cure, and he, in turn, donated it to Shinju-an, where it was taken and rebuilt in 1638, the same year in which its *hōjō* was constructed. A tea room, named the Tei'gyoku-ken, was built on to the north-east corner of the Tsūsen-in by the seventeenth-century tea master and Zen Buddhist monk Kanamori Shigechika, known as Sōwa. He was the eldest son of a *daimyō* (feudal lord), but he was disinherited by his father. He moved with his mother to Kyōto, underwent religious instruction at Daitoku-ji and succeeded in establishing himself as a tea master. He developed an elegant and graceful unique style, which became very popular among the Kyōto aristocracy of his day. It was known as the *hime-Sōwa* (Princess style), in contrast to the style adopted by Sen no Rikyū's grandson Sen no Sōtan, whose Spartan approach got the nickname *kojiki-Sōtan* (Beggar style).

More stepping stones lead from the gate in the garden wall – where, in accordance with the tradition of tea gardens, there is a *secchin* (symbolic privy) – to a stone step in front of the veranda of the Tsūsen-in, then on to the entrance of the Tei'gyoku-ken tea room. The Tsūsen-in can also be accessed from the *hōjō* by means of a roofed corridor, which is provided with a bench and a stone basin.

A view of the garden from the Tsūsen-in (far left); the Tei'gyoku-ken tea room seen from the service entrance – with seating for the host on the left (left); the tea room has a tiny vestibule (with its own stone basin), which takes the place of an inner tea garden (below left).

The garden facing the Tsūsen-in at Shinju-an has a double purpose. It serves as an approach to the Tei'gyoku-ken tea room, but was also designed to be viewed and appreciated from the main *shoin* (reception hall) of the Tsūsen-in itself. The main features of the garden – a tall stone lantern, a superb *sute-ishi* (standing stone) and several specimen trees, including *Ternstroemia gymnanthera* and *Vaccinium bracteatum* – are presented crisply against the bareness of the garden wall, which forms its backdrop. The effect is very much like the *zanzan jōsui* style of ink-brush painting, where much of the painting is left blank. This is an elegant and refined garden, which is extremely intimate at the same time as it preserves an air of a dignified formality.

The Tei'gyoku-ken possesses a very distinctive feature: a tiny vestibule with its own stone water basin. The vestibule serves as the inner *roji* (tea garden) (although it is covered by a roof) and provides an area where guests can tidy themselves before entering the tea room.

The addition of a vestibule was Sōwa's nod to the land of his birth – he came from the mountainous Hida-takayama region of modern-day Gifu prefecture, where it snows heavily in winter.

The south garden of Keishun-in's *hōjō* is called the Shinnyo-no-niwa (Garden of *Tathatā*). *Tathatā* is a Buddhist concept signifying 'the state of things as they are'. The positioning of the modestly sized stones follows the style seen in the east garden of the *hōjō* at Shinju-an, only here the stones are set among camellias, maples, a Kirishima azalea (*Rhododendron obtusum*) and an ancient *Pieris japonica*.

KEISHUN-IN

The tea ceremony was immensely popular at Daitoku-ji, but Myōshin-ji was different. It was strict about spiritual discipline and frowned on activities that might distract their monks from their meditation exercises. Poetry gatherings, incense appreciation gatherings and *nōh* plays were all banned, along with the tea ceremony, and there was even a cell where offenders were incarcerated. This meant that any tea rooms created at Myōshin-ji were discreetly tucked away in odd corners. At Taizō-in, for example, the only indications that it possesses a tea room are a stone basin and a narrow row of stepping stones running along the west front of the *hōjō* (abbot's hall) and past the *kare-sansui* (dry-landscape) garden traditionally attributed to Kanō Motonobu. This path then turns a corner and leads to the entrance of the tea room, which is hidden around the north side of the *hōjō* building.

Keishun-in was one of the very few *tacchū* (sub-temples) at Myōshin-ji that was allowed to have a tea room, and, even so, the tea room in question is situated tactfully behind shrubbery around the side of the *shoin* (reception hall). The shrubbery, however, provided an excuse for landscaping the area surrounding both the *hōjō* and the *shoin* in a unified woodland style, and Keishun-in's gardens are, in fact, a sophisticated interpretation of Sen no Rikyū's style of *roji* (tea garden).

This sub-temple was originally founded in 1598 as Kenshō-in by Oda Hidenori, a grandson of the warlord Oda Nobunaga. In 1632, the military commander Ishikawa Sadamasa took it over, renamed it Keishun-in, in memory of his parents, and built the present *hōjō* and *kuri* (domestic quarters). It is believed that Keishun-in was given special dispensation to have a tea room because of Sadamasa, and that the Kihaku-an tea room was brought here either from Sadamasa's Nagahama Castle together with the *shoin* building, or separately from another residence in his possession. In 1615, the Tokugawa shogunate decided to reduce the overall number of castles in Japan, and Nagahama Castle, on the shores of Lake Biwa, was one of many that were torn down at that time.

Keishun-in is situated on the north-east edge of Myōshin-ji's temple complex, and its buildings are perched on a slight elevation – the ground sloping away to the east and south of the *hōjō* (abbot's hall). The *hōjō* faces south according to the usual custom, and the *genkan* (formal entrance) with a porch is located near the west end of the *hōjō*'s long south veranda. The *genkan* is no longer in use, but the first thing important visitors to the temple would have seen before stepping up on to the veranda was the glorious 'waterfall' of Satsuki azaleas (*Rhododendron indicum*), which covers the embankment separating the *hōjō* from the south garden. Satsuki azaleas have been thickly planted here and clipped to form a single mass, like a sheet of falling water.

The south garden of the *hōjō* is a narrow rectangular moss garden with relatively modest-sized stones, set among fine specimen trees including Japanese maples, a Kirishima azalea (*Rhododendron obtusum*) and *asebi* (*Pieris japonica*). It backs on to a tall clipped evergreen hedge. This garden is meant to be viewed from the *hōjō*, but there is a path leading from the *genkan* around the back of the hedge and through a moss-carpeted grove with handsome, well-grown trees. By a *koi* pond, the path turns northwards. To its right, there is an exceedingly plain, wooden gate – another entrance into the grounds of the sub-temple. Near this gate stands a well in the middle of a small clearing among the trees. From here, stepping stones proceed through a thicket of trees and

shrubs towards the *hōjō*'s east garden. The terrain here has been varied with hillocks. The path continues up a slope to the veranda of the *hōjō*, while another set of stepping stones veers off to the right by a *zazen* (sitting meditation) stone and a stone lantern, and leads up a different slope to a roofed wooden gateway.

The garden to this gateway serves as the Kihaku-an tea room's outer *roji* (tea garden). Beyond the gate is the middle *roji*. This is a very simple garden featuring beautiful stepping stones set among the moss. These go to a low, diagonal-lattice gate constructed of bamboo canes. The lattice gate, in turn, opens on to the inner *roji* (tea garden), the tiny forecourt of the Kihaku-an tea room. This forecourt, which has a beautiful small stone basin tucked into

OPPOSITE A path lies through a grove of mature trees behind the south *hōjō* garden (left); this well in a clearing near the east entrance into the garden has adjacent stepping stones leading leftwards towards the east garden of the *hōjō* (right).

ABOVE Stepping stones cross the east *hōjō* garden, which serves as the outer *roji* for the Kihaku-an tea room (left); this rustic gate, located at the north end of the east garden, is the entrance to the middle *roji* (right).

BELOW The gate connecting the outer and middle *roji* (tea gardens) at Keishun-in is an example of a traditional tea-garden style of gate known as a *baiken-mon* ('plum-viewing gate'). Stepping stones to the left (though not visible here) lead to a hedge where a tiny bamboo gate opens on to the inner *roji*, which serves as the forecourt to the Kihaku-an tea room.

OPPOSITE This twentieth-century courtyard garden set between the *kuri* (domestic quarters) and the *hōjō* (abbot's hall) features an ancient wellhead. Beside it is a *sanzon-seki* (three sacred stones) arrangement that doubles as a dry waterfall, with gravel symbolising a stream.

one of its corners, is utterly concealed among shrubs and trees.

Both the outer and middle *roji* have been designed not only as tea gardens for guests to pass through, but also as ornamental gardens to be viewed from the temple buildings. The middle *roji* faces the east side of the *shoin* (reception hall), and, if it were not for the diminutive lattice bamboo gate, one would not guess that anything of importance lay behind the shrubbery on that side of the garden.

The Kihaku-an tea room lies to the north of the *shoin* and is separated from it by a narrow corridor. A door from the *shoin* leads into this corridor, where there is a *fusuma* (sliding partition wall) that opens on to the tea room. This was the service entrance, used by the host during the tea ceremony. But such was the secrecy with which the tea room was surrounded that a bookshelf formerly stood in front of the *fusuma*, to conceal its presence.

The tea room is said to have been a favourite of the eminent, seventeenth-century tea master Fujimura Yōken, who was a proponent of Sen no Rikyū's *wabi-cha* (rustic style of tea ceremony). The three *roji* at Keishun-in are very much in sympathy with Rikyū's approach to tea. They have an air of artlessness about them but, at the same time, their rural ambience has been carefully designed and executed.

BELOW A view from Tōfuku-ji's famous bridge, the Tsūten-kyō, over the ravine, which cuts through the grounds of the temple.

OPPOSITE The steep banks of the ravine at Tōfuku-ji are thickly planted with many varieties of Japanese maple (*Acer palmatum*), as well as with the trident maple (*A. buergerianum*), which is native to China and Taiwan but has been long cultivated in Japan.

PLANTS

The custom of planting cherry trees in the garden for their early spring blossoms became established in Japan around the ninth century. The gardens of early Zen Buddhist temples such as Saihō-ji, which still retained an element of the pleasure garden about them, possessed ornamental trees of this kind. At the ancient Kyōto temple Tōfuku-ji, however, all the cherry trees were chopped down sometime towards the end of the fourteenth or the beginning of the fifteenth century. This was done on the orders of Yoshida Minchō, who is now principally remembered as an artist, but he was also a Zen Buddhist monk and an official at Tōfuku-ji with responsibilities for the administration of its buildings. Nearly five centuries later, in 1869, the 288th abbot of Tōfuku-ji followed Minchō's example by having, this time, all the temple's maples cut down. The reason was the same on both occasions — the trees were proving too much of a distraction.

Despite this clearance, Tōfuku-ji was — and still is — famous for its maple trees. A deep ravine runs through the extensive grounds of the temple, and hundreds of Japanese maples were planted along its banks, along with a variety of Trident maple, *Acer buergerianum*, known in Japanese as *tō-kaede*. This was in honour of Tōfuku-ji's founding abbot Enni Bennen, who had spent six years studying in China.

Since the seventeenth century, the ravine has been one of the most popular spots for the denizens of Kyōto to come and enjoy the autumn leaves. Despite the efforts of the nineteenth-century abbot, the maples have since returned in all their glory and so have the crowds — in such numbers that, during November, traffic wardens need to be positioned all along the roads leading to the temple. Very few cherry trees, however, have ever been planted to replace those cut down in the days of Yoshida Minchō.

The camellia in the north garden of
Ryōgen-in's *hōjō* (abbot's hall) has
been clipped with straight edges to
serve as a contrast to the dome-
shaped azaleas.

The debate still rages on, particularly about cherry trees. Are they not perhaps too showy for a temple setting, making people think about temporal pleasures rather than reflect on the state of their souls? It is true that surviving, seventeenth-century gardens in the *kare-sansui* (dry-landscape) style are mainly planted with evergreens, but even they are not altogether devoid of flowering shrubs. Both *Camellia japonica* and *C. sasanqua* are extensively used, largely because they are so amenable to heavy pruning, but also for their delicate blossoms. While a riot of colour was certainly not the desired effect, the flowers awaken a sharp delight in the changing seasons, and they poignantly mark the inevitable passage of time. *Stewartia pseudocamellia* is popularly known in Japan as *shara-no-ki* or sal tree (the true sal tree of India not being hardy enough for the Japanese climate). It produces a flush of ethereal white blossoms for a few weeks in June and early July.

Many *kare-sansui*-style gardens incorporate clipped evergreen shrubs to offset their standing stones. Since the seventeenth century, the Satsuki azalea (*Rhododendron indicum*) has become by far the favourite shrub for this purpose, and it has introduced more colour into these gardens. Not only do its tiny leaves and dense growth make it ideal for pruning, but it produces attractive, dark salmon-pink to orange-pink flowers late in May. At Raikyū-ji in the city of Takahashi in Okayama prefecture, these azaleas are used *en masse* to create towering banks of greenery, which are clipped to represent ocean waves. They form a brilliant contrast against the garden's raked white gravel. More swirling banks of meticulously trimmed azaleas encircle a group of stones representing a crane 'island' and another comprising a turtle 'island'. This garden is thought to have been designed by Kobori Enshū sometime around 1614, when he was staying at this temple while overseeing the restoration of the local castle, which he had inherited from his father. Shigemori Mirei created a similar feature out of the azaleas planted alongside the garden he did for the Tōfuku-ji sub-temple Kōmyō-in.

At **Raikyū-ji** in the town of Takahashi in Okayama prefecture, Kobori Enshū used banks of azaleas in order to create a pattern representing ocean waves (top left); the many varieties of azalea collected from around Japan by the abbot of Kōmyō-in were clipped by Shigemori Mirei into curved banks, symbolising clouds (bottom left). Satsuki azaleas (*Rhododendron indicum*) bloom in late May in the north garden of Ryōgen-in's *hōjō* (bottom right); instead of azaleas, pine trees were once planted along the bank to the rear of the south garden of the *hōjō* at Shūon-an (top right).

Even with non-flowering evergreens, there have been changes in fashion. *Maki* (*Podocarpus macrophyllus*) began to appear in the garden in the thirteenth century, along with Hinoki cypress (*Chamaecyparis obtusa*), a forest tree that had long been valued for its fragrant and strong timber. In the sixteenth century, broadleaved evergreens such as *Photinia glabra*, *Eurya japonica* and various evergreen oaks (such as *Quercus acuta*, *Q. glauca* and *Q. phillyreoides*) became popular, especially for use in mixed hedging, alongside *Camellia sasanqua*, *Cleyera japonica*, *Ardisia japonica*, *Ligustrum japonicum*, *Aucuba japonica*, *Nandina domestica* and the dwarf gardenia *Gardenia jasminoides* among others. By mixing plants in a hedge or in a single large clipped mound, it was possible to create a gradation of colours and textures, as well as leaf sizes, and there was the added benefit of a scattering of flowers and different coloured berries, according to the season.

The favourite berrying plant in Japanese Zen gardens, however, is probably *manryō* (*Ardisia crenata*). It has very glossy, dark green, oval leaves under which, in the autumn and through the winter, it bears deep crimson berries in panicles. *Farfugium japonicum* produces large round leathery leaves (which can be variegated with yellow spots) and, in late autumn, sulphur-yellow flowers borne at the ends of tall stalks. Both plants look superb against moss.

The sago palms (*Cycas revoluta*) in the south garden of the *hōjō* (abbot's hall) at Shūon-an are very effective in introducing an exotic touch to the composition of the garden. This palm is, in fact, native to Japan, being found in

OPPOSITE Here in the south *hōjō* garden of Funda-in, the red-tinged new growth on the photinia contrasts with the mixed evergreen hedge, which includes *Eurya japonica, Ligustrum japonicum, Cleyera japonica* and *Elaeagnus pungens*. There is a row of clipped specimen trees behind the crane and turtle islands, including *Podocarpus macrophyllus*, a conifer often seen in Japanese gardens.

THIS PAGE The smooth bark of the crepe myrtle (*Lagerstroemia indica*), seen here in the east garden at Tenju-an, makes it a very attractive garden tree all year round (below); *Farfugium*

japonicum and *Ardisia crenata*, with red berries, add detail to the east garden at Tenju-an (below right); Japanese beauty berry (*Callicarpa japonica*) is thought to have originally been called *murasaki-shikimi* (purple berry bush) in Japanese, but it is now known by the name of the famous author of *The Tale of Genji, murasaki-shikibu* (right).

FOLLOWING SPREAD A splendid sago palm (*Cycas revoluta*) provides a touch of exoticism to the south *hōjō* garden of Shūon-an (left); haircap moss (*Polytrichum* spp.) is known in Japan as *sugi-goke*, because of its resemblance to the needles of Japanese cedar (*Cryptomeria japonica*) (right).

the far south of the island of Kyūshū, but it appears to have been introduced into Kyōto during the fifteenth century through the trade with China. Although it is recorded as having been planted in gardens at the time, sago palm became popular only in the sixteenth and seventeenth centuries, with the emergence of a general taste for the flamboyant in the visual arts. Even Zen Buddhist gardens were not immune to the exuberance of the age.

Perhaps the most surprisingly temperamental of all plants is moss, which crops up where it is not wanted and shrivels up where it is. Where moss is happy, different species will colonise the ground, stones and trunks of trees. For the Japanese, moss is an important symbol of the passage of time, and it even appears in the national anthem.

The type of moss most frequently encountered in gardens is *sugi-goke*, named after the resemblance of its tiny leaves to the needles on *Cryptomeria japonica*. *Sugi-goke* is what is known in English as haircap moss. Species belonging to the *Rhizogonium* genus, with their soft, brush-like appearance, are known as *itachi-no-shippo-goke* (weasel's tail moss) or *hinoki-goke*, after the Hinoki cypress. Then there is *Leucoloma molle*, known in Japanese as *matsuba-goke* (pine-needle moss).

This is the enduring attraction of Japanese Zen temple gardens. While standing in an urban garden, you may come across Shumisen – the centre of the Buddhist universe. Or you may discover a dense, mysterious, primeval forest in a clump of moss. All you have to do is look.

VISITING TEMPLES

ADDRESSES AND OPENING TIMES

The *hōjō* (abbot's hall) of a Zen Buddhist temple will generally have a shrine located in its *shicchū* (central room). At many temples, this shrine is dedicated to a statue or painting of the temple's founding abbot, in keeping with the Zen Buddhist tradition of revering the founding abbot as an ever-present member of the temple community and as its head teacher. At others, the shrine in the *hōjō* is dedicated to the Buddha – usually the Gautama Buddha, but occasionally to a different Buddha. The etiquette for a Buddhist is to offer a prayer in front of the shrine before turning around to contemplate the garden.

It is considered irreverent to turn one's back to the shrine. Hence, the *hōjō*'s main garden is usually designed to be appreciated mainly from one or another of the reception rooms on either side of the *shicchū*, although the view from the *shicchū* – where the founding abbot, symbolically speaking, sits in eternal contemplation of the garden – would also have been taken into consideration.

The *hōjō*'s style of architecture is basically domestic, and people sit on the tatami matting in the formal *seiza* (kneeling) position, with their knees tucked under them. Gardens are, therefore, designed to be viewed from this angle, not a standing position. Some temples allow members of the public to enter their *hōjō* or *shoin* (reception hall); others do not, in which case the garden has to be viewed from the veranda.

Sandals are frequently provided at temples that allow visitors to stroll through parts of their garden. These should be removed before returning to the veranda. The Japanese do not wear shoes inside their homes, and the principle applies to a Zen temple's *hōjō*, *shoin* and the living areas of the *kuri* (domestic quarters). The veranda, moreover, is considered to be 'indoors' and should not be trodden on with outdoor footwear.

A monk attends to his morning duties at Nanzen-ji.

(Please note that temples charge admission to buildings and gardens. They may be closed for special ceremonies and private services. Some Kyōto temples that are normally closed to the public may open for a limited number of days in the spring or autumn.)

DAISEN-IN (sub-temple of Daitoku-ji)
54-1 Murasakino Daitokuji-chō, Kita-ku, Kyōto-shi 603-8231
(075) 491-8346
9:00–17:00 (March–November);
9:00–16:30 (December–February)

DAISHIN-IN (sub-temple of Myōshin-ji)
57 Hanazono Myōshinji-chō, Ukyō-ku, Kyōto-shi 616-8035
(075) 461-5714
9:00–17:00 (year-round)

DAITOKU-JI (*DAI-HŌJŌ*)
53 Murasakino Daitokuji-chō, Kita-ku, Kyōto-shi 603-8231
(Usually closed to the public)

EIHŌ-JI
1-42 Kokeizan-chō, Tajimi-shi, Gifu-ken 507-0014
(0572) 22-0351
9:00–17:00 (only closed 1–7 December)

ENKŌ-JI
13 Ichijōji Otani-chō, Sakyō-ku, Kyōto-shi 600-8147
(075) 781-8025
9:00–16:30 (reservation necessary during November; only closed 28–31 December)

ENTSŪ-JI
389 Iwakura Hataeda-chō, Sakyō-ku, Kyōto-shi 606-0015
(075) 781-1875
10:00–16:30 (April–November);
10:00–16:00 (December–March)

ENTOKU-IN
530 Kōdaiji Shimogawara-chō, Higashiyama-ku, Kyōto-shi 605-0825
(075) 525-0101
10:00–17:00; last entry 16:30 (year-round)

FUNDA-IN (sub-temple of Tōfuku-ji, also known as Sesshū-ji)
15-803 Honmachi, Higashiyama-ku, Kyōto-shi 605-0981

(075) 541-1761
9:00–17:00 (March–November);
9:00–16:00 (December–February)

JIKŌ-IN
865 Koizumi-chō, Yamato-kōriyama-shi, Nara-ken 639-1042
(0743) 53-3004
9:00–17:00 (year-round)

JISHŌ-JI (GINKAKU-JI)
2 Ginkakuji-chō, Sakyō-ku, Kyōto-shi 606-8402
(075) 771-5725
8:30–17:00 (March–November);
9:00–16:30 (December–February)

JŌEI-JI
2001 Miyanoshita, Yamaguchi-shi, Yamaguchi-ken 753-0011
(083) 922-2272
8:00–17:00; last entry 16:30 (April–September);
8:00–16:30; last entry 16:00 (October–March)

KEISHUN-IN (sub-temple of Myōshin-ji)
11 Hanazono Teranonaka-chō, Ukyō-ku, Kyōto-shi 616-8036
(075) 463-6578
9:00–17:00 (year-round)

KENNIN-JI
584 Komatsu-chō, Higashiyama-ku, Kyōto-shi 605-0811
(075) 561-6363
10:00–16:00 (only closed 20 April, 4–5 June, 28-31 December)

KŌDAI-JI
526 Kōdaiji Shimogawara-chō, Higashiyama-ku, Kyōto-shi 605-0825
(075) 561-9966
9:00–17:00 (year-round)

KOHŌ-AN (sub-temple of Daitoku-ji)
66 Murasakino Daitokuji-chō, Kita-ku, Kyōto-shi 603-8231
(Closed to the public)

KŌMYŌ-IN (sub-temple of Tōfuku-ji)
15-809 Honmachi, Higashiyama-ku, Kyōto-shi 605-0981
(075) 561-7317
8:30–sunset (year-round)

KONCHI-IN (sub-temple of Nanzen-ji)
86-12 Nanzenji Fukuchi-chō, Sakyō-ku, Kyōto-shi 606-8435
(075) 771-3511
8:30–17:00 (March–November);
8:30–16:30 (December–February)

KŌTŌ-IN (sub-temple of Daitoku-ji)
73-1 Murasakino Daitokuji-chō, Kita-ku, Kyōto-shi 603-8231
(075) 492-0068
9:00–16:30 (only closed 6 May, 7–8 June)

MANPUKU-JI
25-33 Higashimachi, Masuda-shi, Shimane-ken 698-004
(0856) 22-0302
8:00–17:00 (year-round)

NANZEN-JI (*DAI-HŌJŌ* AND *KO-HŌJŌ*) AND NANZEN-IN
Nanzenji Fukuchi-chō, Sakyō-ku, Kyōto-shi 606-8435
(075) 771-0365
8:40–17:00; last entry 16:40 (March–November);
8:40–16:30; last entry 16:10 (December–February but closed 28–31 December)

ŌBAI-IN (sub-temple of Daitoku-ji)
83-1 Murasakino Daitokuji-chō, Kita-ku, Kyōto-shi 603-8231
(075) 492-4539
10:00–16:00 (for several weeks in April and November)

RAIKYŪ-JI
18 Raikyūji-chō, Takahashi-shi, Okayama-ken 716-0016
(0866) 22-3516
9:00–17:00 (year-round)

REUIN-IN (sub-temple at Myōshin-ji)
39 Hanazono Myōshinji-chō, Ukyō-ku, Kyōto-shi 616-8035
Closed to the public

ROKUŌ-IN
24 Saga Kitabori-chō, Ukyō-ku, Kyōto-shi 616-8367
(075) 861-1645
9:00–17:00 (year-round)

ROKUON-JI (KINKAKU-JI)
1 Kinkakuji-chō, Kita-ku, Kyōto-shi 603-8361
(075) 461-0013
9:00–17:00 (year-round)

RYŌAN-JI
13 Ryōanji Goryōnoshita-chō, Ukyō-ku,
Kyōto-shi 616-8001
(075) 463-2216
8:00–17:00 (March–November);
8:30–16:30 (December–February)

RYŌGEN-IN (sub-temple of Daitoku-ji)
82-1 Murasakino Daitokuji-chō, Kita-ku,
Kyōto-shi 603-8231
(075) 491-7635
9:00–16:30 (year-round)

RYŌGIN-AN (sub-temple of Tōfuku-ji)
15 Honmachi, Higashiyama-ku, Kyōto-shi 605-0981
(075) 561-0087
9:00–16:00 (only 14–16 March and during November)

SAIHŌ-JI (Koke-dera, the Moss Temple)
56 Matsuō Jingatani-chō, Nishikyō-ku,
Kyōto-shi 615-8286
(075) 391-3631
(Write, sending a stamped return postcard (from inside
Japan) or a self-addressed envelope (from abroad), to
book a reservation at least seven days in advance of
your visit, giving your name and address, the number of
people in your group and proposed date of visit.)

SHINJU-AN (sub-temple of Daitoku-ji)
52 Murasakino Daitokuji-chō, Kita-ku,
Kyōto-shi 603-8231
(Closed to the public)

SHŌDEN-JI
72 Nishigamo Kitachinjuan-chō, Kita-ku,
Kyōto-shi 603-8847
(075) 491-3259
9:00–17:00 (year-round)

SHŪON-AN (popularly known as Ikkyū-ji)
102 Makisatonouchi, Kyō-tanabe-shi,
Kyōto-fu 610-0341
(0774) 62-0193
9:00–17:00 (year-round)
(Ikkyū Sōjun's hermitage and mausoleum are closed
to the public)

TAIZŌ-IN (sub-temple of Myōshin-ji)
35 Hanazono Myōshinji-chō, Ukyō-ku,
Kyōto-shi 616-8035
(075) 463-2855
9:00–17:00 (special reservation required to view the
west garden from inside the *hōjō*)

TENJU-AN (sub-temple of Nanzen-ji)
86-8 Nanzenji Fukuchi-chō, Sakyō-ku,
Kyōto-shi 606-8435
(075) 771-0744
9:00–17:00 (spring–autumn, but closed
11–12 November);
9:00–16:30 (winter)

TENRYŪ-JI
68 Susukinobaba-chō, Saga Tenryūji, Ukyō-ku,
Kyōto-shi 616-8385
(075) 881-1235
8:30–17:30 (21 March–20 October);
8:30–17:00 (21 October–20 March)

TŌFUKU-JI
15-778 Honmachi, Higashiyama-ku,
Kyōto-shi 605-0981
(075) 561-0087
9:00–16:00 (year-round; separate admission for the
hōjō and for the Kaisan-dō/Fumon-in garden)

TŌKAI-AN (sub-temple of Myōshin-ji)
61 Hanazono Myōshinji-chō, Ukyō-ku,
Kyōto-shi 616-8035
(Closed to the public)

TŌKŌ-JI
3-7-37 Tōkōji-chō, Kōfu-shi, Yamanashi-ken 400-0805
(052) 233-9070
9:00–17:00 (year-round)

ZAKKE-IN (sub-temple of Myōshin-ji)
55 Hanazono Myōshinji-chō, Ukyō-ku,
Kyōto-shi 616-8035
(Closed to the public)

ZUIHŌ-IN (sub-temple of Daitoku-ji)
81 Murasakino Daitokuji-chō, Kita-ku,
Kyōto-shi 603-8231
(075) 491-1454
9:00–17:00 (year-round)

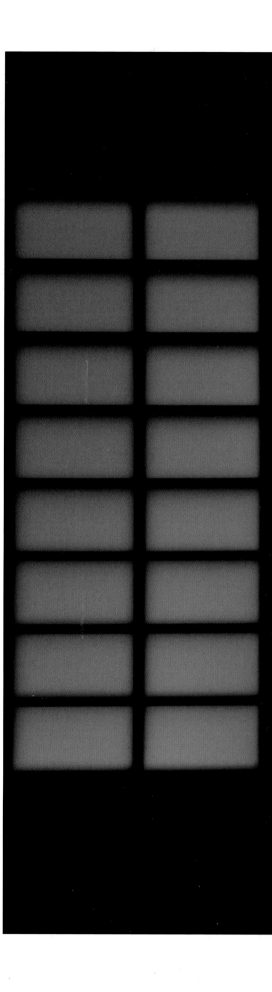

Ladies with parasols walk past the red columns of
Daitoku-ji's *sanmon* (main inner gateway).

OTHER SIGNIFICANT BUDDHIST TEMPLE GARDENS

GENKŌ-AN

47 Takagamine Kita-takagamine-chō, Kita-ku,
Kyōto-shi 603-8468
(075) 492-1858
9:00–17:00 (year-round; reservation required for
Saturdays, Sundays and public holidays)
The main hall of this Sōtō temple possesses two
famous windows: a square one, representing man's
spiritual weaknesses; and a round window, symbolising
enlightenment. The building dates back to c.1694.

JIZŌ-IN

23 Yamada Kitanomachi, Nishikyō-ku,
Kyōto-shi 615-8285
(075) 381-3417
9:00–17:00 (April–November);
9:00–16:30 (December–March)
This temple, originally founded in 1367, is located near
Saihō-ji. The present hōjō, built in 1686, looks out on
to a moss garden known as the Garden of the Sixteen
Rakan (although it has more than sixteen stones).
The temple is famous for its bamboo groves and a
magnificent kochō wabisuke camellia, which produces
small, bell-shaped, variegated flowers in mid-March.

JUKŌ-IN (sub-temple of Daitoku-ji)

58 Murasakino Daitokuji-chō, Kita-ku,
Kyōto-shi 603-8231
(Closed to the public but occasionally open for
special viewing)
The grave of the celebrated tea master Sen no Rikyū
is located at this Daitoku-ji sub-temple, founded in
1566. The south garden of its hōjō is said to have
been designed by Rikyū; another tradition is that this
kare-sansui garden, representing the turtle and the
crane, complements the fusuma paintings in the
shicchū of the hōjō. The paintings by Kanō Eitoku
represent an autumnal scene, a winter scene and a
spring scene: summer is supposed to be portrayed
by the garden itself. The lotus pond depicted on one
of the fusuma is supposed symbolically to feed the
'ocean', symbolised by the white Shirakawa gravel with
which the garden is formerly thought to have been laid.
Both of these theories remain conjectures, however.

KŌRIN-IN (sub-temple of Daitoku-ji)

80 Murasakino Daitokuji-chō, Kita-ku,
Kyōto-shi 603-8231
(075) 491-7636
(Open for special viewing in the spring and in
the autumn)
Founded c.1530, this Daitoku-ji sub-temple features a
kare-sansui garden representing Mt Hōrai. The garden
was recreated from old records in the late 1970s by
Nakane Kinsaku.

MYŌREN-JI

875 Myōrenji-mae, Kamigyō-ku, Kyōto-shi 602-8418
(075) 451-3527
10:00–16:00 (year-round, but closed Wednesdays and
around New Year's Eve and New Year's Day)
This head temple of a branch of the Nichiren-Hokkei
sect of Japanese Buddhism possesses a superb
kare-sansui garden representing the Sixteen Rakan. It is
said to have been created by the monk Gyokuen, who
belonged to this temple.

NANSHŪ-JI

3-1-2 Minami-hatago-chō Higashi, Sakai-ku, Sakai-shi,
Ōsaka-fu 590-0965
(072) 232-1654
9:00–16:00 (year-round)
This important Rinzai Zen temple in the city of Sakai
has a garden traditionally said to have been designed
by the tea master Furuta Oribe. The temple, however,
was relocated to its present site in 1615, the year in
which Oribe died. The garden, a delicate kare-sansui
depicting a waterfall and river, was badly damaged in a
Second World War bombing raid, but was restored by
the garden historian Mori Osamu.

REIKAN-JI

12 Shishigatani Goshonodan-chō, Sakyō-ku,
Kyōto-shi 606-8422
(075) 771-4040
10:00–16:00 (for a week in April and in November)
This temple, founded in 1687 by a daughter of the
emperor Gosai, features a splendid kare-sansui
garden and is also famous for its camellias and
Japanese maples.

REIUN-IN (sub-temple of Tōfuku-ji)

15-801 Honmachi, Higashiyama-ku,
Kyōto-shi 605-0981
(075) 561-4080
9:00–16:00 (year-round)
Founded c.1390, this sub-temple possessed a garden
representing the mountain ranges and oceans
surrounding Shumisen. Shumisen itself is symbolised
by a famous stone given to the seventh abbot by the
daimyō Hosokawa Tadayoshi, son of the daimyō and
tea master Hosokawa Sansai. The garden was heavily
restored in 1970 by Shigemori Mirei, who also created a
new garden for the west side of the shoin.

SHISEN-DŌ

27 Ichijōji Kadoguchi-chō, Sakyō-ku,
Kyōto-shi 606-8154
(075) 781-2954
9:00–17:00; last entry 16:45 (year-round)
This temple was originally the home of the
seventeenth-century, man-of-letters Ishikawa Jōzan,
who created its beautiful, kare-sansui garden. This
garden was modified in 1748 and restored to its original
design in 1967. Shisen-dō became a Zen Buddhist
temple of the Sōtō school in 1966.

TŌJI-IN

63 Tōjiin Kitamachi, Kita-ku, Kyōto-shi 603-8346
(075) 461-5786
8:00–17:00; last entry 16:30 (only closed
29 December–3 January)
The shogun Ashikaga Taka'uji founded this temple as
Kita-tōji-ji in 1341, appointing Musō Soseki as its first
abbot. It became the family temple of the Ashikaga
clan. The east pond garden is traditionally said to
have been created by Musō. The west pond garden
was heavily restored during the eighteenth century;
it is overlooked by a teahouse supposedly built by
the shogun Ashikaga Yoshimasa in 1458, but much
modified in later centuries, with an annexe attached
in 1896.

GLOSSARY OF TERMS

aoishi: the term by which chlorite schist is popularly known in Japanese. This metamorphic rock is highly prized in Japan for use in the garden. It is found on the island of Shikoku as well as along the river Kinokawa, near the city of Wakayama to the south of Ōsaka. Quarrying this stone is now prohibited in Wakayama.

bonsan: the art of creating a miniature landscape in a container using stones to represent mountains and fine gravel to symbolise the sea, as well as miniature trees.

bonseki: the art of presenting a fine specimen rock in a container. Also known as *bonkei*.

Buddha: 'the Enlightened One'. Siddhartha Gautama (also known as the Shakyamuni Buddha) is the historical Buddha, the spiritual teacher who was born an Indian prince sometime in the fourth or fifth century BC. Various schools belonging to the Mahāyāna branch of Buddhism (which spread from India to Tibet, China, Korea and Japan, as well as south to Vietnam, Sri Lanka, Indonesia and Malaysia) have a devotion to other manifestations of Buddha, existing in the past, present and future. Among them are the *Amida-nyorai*, the Amida Buddha (Amitābha in Sanskrit), the *Yakushi-nyorai* (Bhaisajyaguru) and the Miroku Bosatsu (Maitreya), the Buddha to come in the future.

bushi: a member of the warrior class in Japan, which existed from the tenth century to the mid-nineteenth century. The term *samurai* came to designate members of this class only in the sixteenth century and was initially used of high-ranking military retainers of the ruling classes.

busshō: Buddha nature (*Buddha-dhātu* in Sanskrit). One of the teachings of the Mahāyāna branch of Buddhism is that all human beings share the potential to attain spiritual enlightenment. Under the influence of Chinese Daoism, *busshō* was extended to all things – both living and inanimate.

Chán Buddhism: the Chinese term for Zen Buddhism.

daimyō: feudal regional lords who had governorship over their domains. Their precise status changed over the centuries; under the Tokugawa shogunate, the term was applied to the hereditary governors of the wealthier of the numerous fiefdoms into which the regime divided the country.

Daoism: a school of Chinese philosophical and religious beliefs incorporating the teachings attributed to the philosophers Laozi and Zhuangzi; it also taught a complex cosmology and a system of influences believed to govern the natural world.

enzan-seki: a stone, usually triangular in shape, placed at the head of a dry waterfall stone arrangement to suggest the view of a far-off mountain rising up behind the waterfall.

Hōrai (Mt Pénglái in Chinese): this is the most important of the Islands of the Immortals – the home of immortal sages, according to Daoist beliefs. The other islands are Hōjō (Fāngzhàng in Chinese) and Eishū (Yíngzhōu). Two more islands – Taiyo (Dàiyú) and Inkyō (Yuánjiāo) – were believed to have been swept away in a tidal wave.

Fudō-myo'ō (Acalanātha in Sanskrit): a male figure usually portrayed in Buddhist art with a fierce visage, holding an upright sword in his right hand and surrounded by flames. He is believed to be a guardian of all those who are undergoing spiritual training and who seek enlightenment. He has been particularly revered in Japan.

fusuma: a panel consisting of a wooden frame covered with heavy opaque paper or cloth. *Fusuma* run on rails and make up partition walls in traditional Japanese buildings. They can be removed so that rooms can be opened up to create bigger spaces.

genkan: the formal entrance to a building. The *genkan* of a Zen temple *hōjō* can either be part of the building itself or a separate gateway, often with an additional porch.

hattō: the lecture or sermon hall of a large Zen Buddhist temple.

hira-niwa: a term that came into use in the eighteenth century to refer to level gravelled gardens that were landscaped with stones and plants.

hōjō: the abbot's hall. Where there are two such buildings, they are sometimes distinguished as the *dai-hōjō* (large hall) and the *ko-hōjō* (small hall).

hon-dō: the main hall of a Buddhist temple, containing the temple's central shrine to the Buddha. It is also referred to as the *butsu-den*. At some Zen Buddhist temples, the *hon-dō* is a *hōjō*-style building. Conversely, a temple may have only a *hōjō*, and this houses the shrine.

Jōdo: shortened form of *Gokuraku Jōdo* (Paradise of the Pure Land) or *Saihō Jōdo* (Pure Land of the West). It is the realm inhabited by the Amida Buddha.

jōkō: abbreviated form of the title *daijō-tennō*, which was given to an abdicated *tennō* (emperor). From the last decades of the eleventh century onwards, several emperors abdicated in favour of their young heirs so that they might be liberated from the ceremonial functions of the emperorship and be more free to wield political influence.

Kannon Bosatsu: the Indian bodhisattva Avalokiteśvara, long venerated in Japan. In Japanese Buddhist art, the Kannon Bosatsu and the Seishi Bosatsu (the bodhisattva Mahāsthāmaprāpta) are the two traditional attendants on the Amida Buddha.

kare-sansui: a dry-landscape garden. It is dry in the sense that it does not incorporate any water in the form of a stream, river or pond. It can, and frequently is, carpeted with moss. While gravel is generally used to represent water, the moss can also serve this function. The term *sansui* or *senzui* (literally, mountain water) was originally applied to natural landscapes, but by the middle of the fourteenth century, it included landscape gardens as well. The word *kare-sansui* (*kare* meaning 'dry') is used in the eleventh-century garden manual the *Sakutei-ki*, but it does not reappear for a long while, and, for several centuries from the fourteenth century onwards, the term usually seen in written documents is *kari-sansui*. The *kari* in *kari-sansui* can be translated variously as 'makeshift', 'assumed', 'fabricated' or 'temporary'; it suggests that the *kari-sansui* garden is an imitation of, as well as a stand-in for, a real landscape.

kōan: short anecdotes and paradoxical sayings attributed to great Zen masters of the past, which are used especially in Rinzai Zen Buddhism as a spur to meditation.

kuri: the building that traditionally housed the domestic quarters and kitchen of a Zen Buddhist temple.

kyaku-den: the building chiefly containing the reception rooms in which the abbot received his guests and met parishioners and patrons of his temple. At some of the smaller Zen Buddhist temples, the *kyaku-den* takes the form of a *hōjō* and serves also as the *hon-dō*.

mandala: a geometrical diagram setting out the cosmos according to the relationships existing between various Buddhas and bodhisattvas.

mu: 'nothingness' in Japanese. This term is used in Japanese Zen Buddhism as a synonym for *kū* (emptiness), which translates the Sanskrit word *śūnyatā* meaning 'zero' or 'void'. It describes the transient state of all things: there is no thing that has absolute being; everything emerges out of the interaction of various interconnected causes.

nijiri-guchi: a small, square entrance to a tea room, necessitating entry in a kneeling position.

nirvana (*ne'han* in Japanese): the state of calmness attained when all desires, passions and spiritual confusion have been extinguished, and one is finally released from the cycle of death and rebirth.

niwa: : a Japanese term now used to mean 'garden', it was originally applied to the flat open ceremonial space that was located in front of the *shinden* (main hall) of eleventh- and twelfth-century aristocrats' palaces.

rakan (*arakan*; *arhat* in Sanskrit): a holy man who has undergone spiritual training. In Chinese and Japanese Buddhism, there was a tradition of venerating a group of legendary *rakan* – sixteen, eighteen or five hundred in number. The Five Hundred *Rakan* refer to the assembly of Gautama Buddha's disciples who are said to have convened after his death to decide on the canonical sutras.

reihai-seki: worship, or prayer, stone.

roji: the garden that leads to the entrance of a tea room. Originally, the word simply referred to a pathway, but, by the beginning of the eighteenth century, the Buddhist concept of *roji* (literally, the 'dewy ground') was being superimposed on it. The 'dewy ground' is a Buddhist metaphor for the state in which one is free from all passions, desires and sorrows.

ryūmon-baku: literally, a 'dragon-gate waterfall'. It is a waterfall arrangement that includes a *rigyo-seki*, a stone representing a carp attempting to swim up the falls.

sanzon-seki: a style of grouping three stones together in the garden, reflecting the way in which the figure of Buddha is commonly depicted in Buddhist art, flanked on either side by a bodhisattva. A *sanzon-seki* arrangement is often employed in the garden to represent Buddha and his attendants, but not always.

seiza: the formal Japanese style of sitting. It is in a kneeling position, with the legs folded flat under the body, the knees placed close together and the back held straight.

senzui-kawaramono: a member of a semi-outcast social class known as *kawaramono* who specialised in constructing gardens. *Kawaramono* (riverbank people) were so called because they originally lived along riverbanks and engaged in despised occupations such as tanning. *Kawaramono* existed as a distinct social class from around the eleventh century to the early decades of the seventeenth century.

shakkei: borrowed landscape.

shicchū: the central of the three public rooms of a *hōjō*, this was the room in which the abbot imparted religious instruction to his disciples. A shrine dedicated to the temple's founding abbot, to the Buddha, or to both, was usually located to the rear of the *shicchū*. Sometimes, the shrine was ensconced in a small room of its own (the *butsu-ma*), situated at the back of the *shicchū*.

shinden-zukuri: an aristocratic style of architecture predating the appearance of the *shoin*-style room. The *shinden* was the main hall of a complex of buildings interconnected with corridors.

Shirakawa gravel: The gravel used in Japanese gardens is usually referred to in Japanese as *suna* (sand), but the size of the particles is usually much larger than that generally associated these days with sand, either in the West or in Japan. In previous centuries, laying gravel or small pebbles as large as 3–5 cm/1¼–2 inches in diameter was still referred to, among the gardening profession, as 'spreading sand'. *Shirakawa-zuna* (literally, Shirakawa sand) consists of weathered pulverised white granite, which was formerly collected from the upper reaches of the Shirakawa, a relatively short but fast-flowing river running from the foothills of Mt Hiei down to the city of Kyōto. Removing gravel from the Shirakawa has been prohibited since the latter half of the 1950s, and the gravel is now produced by pulverising quarried white granite, of a similar composition to the famous white Shirakawa granite, from near Mt Hiei.

shogun: signifying a general or a military commander, this rank was officially made by court appointment. At certain periods in Japanese history, several shogun existed at the same time. While the Kamakura, Ashikaga and Togukawa regimes were in power, however, the only shogun appointed was the *sei'i-taishōgun*, who was the *de facto* ruler of Japan (although during both the Kamakura and Ashikaga regimes, the authority of the shogun declined so that he became a figurehead much like the emperor himself). Toyotomi Hideyoshi was appointed *kanpaku* (regent), but never *sei'i-taishōgun*, although he unified and governed the country.

shoin: a formal study in a style that emerged during the fourteenth and fifteenth centuries. Architectural innovations included an alcove and a decorative set of staggered shelves; *fusuma* used as partition walls; and a floor fitted entirely with tatami matting. Early *shoin* were used to receive private guests and, before long, the *shoin* was being mainly utilised as a reception room, rather than as a study. The term *shoin* is also applied to the building that houses *shoin*-type rooms.

shōji: a wooden-framed panel covered with either paper or cloth and used as wall partitions. *Fusuma* was originally a type of *shōji*. The term *shōji* is used these days to refer to panels covered with translucent rice paper, which lets diffused light through. In traditional Japanese buildings, a row of sliding *shōji*, fitted into grooved rails, separates individual rooms from the *engawa* (veranda). At night, a set of heavy wooden panels (*amado* or 'rain shutters') is drawn along grooved rails usually located along the outer edge of the *engawa* or, in cases where there is a *nure-en* (outer veranda) as well as an inner one, between the two. These *amado* effectively box in the house, thus providing security. *Shōji* are also fitted in front of windows.

Shumisen: according to ancient Indian cosmological belief, this is the mountain that stands at the centre of the universe. It is surrounded by eight seas alternating with eight rings of mountains. It is known as Sumeru in Sanskrit.

sute-ishi: a prominent stone used by itself (rather than in a grouping) in order to balance the design of the entire garden.

tacchū: a semi-autonomous sub-temple operating under the umbrella of a larger temple.

tatami: a large thick rectangular mat covered with woven rush of a sweet-smelling kind known as *igusa*. Until the latter half of the fifteenth century, houses belonging to the upper echelons of society had wooden flooring; tatami mats were used only where people of the highest rank were expected to sit. With the innovation of the *shoin*, rectangular tatami came to be used to cover the entire floor. A tatami is designed to be twice as long as it is wide; and in Japan the size of a room is even now described according to how many tatami fit into it. Sizes of tatami were standardised from the seventeenth century onwards.

tsukiyama: a man-made garden hillock.

wabi: the aesthetic appreciation of tranquillity mixed with a quiet acceptance of the transcience of all being. *Wabi-cha* is a style of tea ceremony in which a rustic setting is chosen to enhance this sense of *wabi*.

zanzan jōsui (*cán shān shèng shuǐ* in Chinese): a style of ink-brush painting developed by artists of the Southern Song dynasty, in which a landscape is not fully depicted but rather its vastness is suggested by its most salient features, the rest of the painting being left blank. The style was extremely influential in Japan. The term *zanzan jōsui* literally means 'remaining mountains, surviving rivers' and was originally used in China to refer to a landscape desolated by war. It came later to be applied to the severely minimalist style of ink-brush painting in which more is left undepicted than is depicted.

zazen: meditation in a sitting position.

Zen Buddhism: a school of Mahāyāna, one of the two principal branches of Buddhism. The two main traditions of Zen Buddhism in Japan are the Rinzai school, introduced by Myōan Yōsai; and the Sōtō school, which traces its history back to the teachings of the Japanese monk Dōgen, who studied Chán Buddhism in China in the 1220s. While the Sōtō school focuses on sitting meditation, the Rinzai school also uses *kōan* as a means of spiritual training.

INDEX

Page numbers in *italic* refer to illustrations

FURTHER READING

Addiss, Stephen, *The Art of Zen: Paintings and calligraphy by Japanese monks, 1600–1925*, Harry N. Abrams, New York, 1989

Attlee, Helena, *The Gardens of Japan*, Frances Lincoln, London, 2010

Berthier, François, *Reading Zen in the Rocks: The Japanese dry landscape garden*, trans. with essay by Graham Parkes, University of Chicago Press, Chicago and London, 2000

Conder, Josiah, *Landscape Gardening in Japan*, 2nd edn, 1912; reprint, Dover Publications, New York, 1991

Du Cane, Florence, *The Flowers and Gardens of Japan*, Adam & Charles Black, London, 1908; this book is available through print-on-demand publishers Ulan Press

Itoh, Teiji, *Gardens of Japan*, Kodansha International, Tōkyō, New York and London, 2nd edn, 1998

Kawaguchi, Yoko, *Serene Gardens: Creating Japanese design and detail in the Western garden*, New Holland, London, 2nd edn, 2008

Keane, Marc P., *Japanese Garden Design*, Charles E. Tuttle, Tōkyō and Rutland, VT, 2004

Kuitert, Wybe, *Themes in the History of Japanese Garden Art*, University of Hawaii Press, Honolulu, 2002

Muso Kokushi and Thomas Cleary, *Dream Conversations: On Buddhism and Zen* (trans. of Musō Soseki's *Muchū mondōshū*), Shambhala Publications, Boston and London, 1996

Nomura, Kanji (ed.), *Kobori Enshu: A tea master's harmonic brilliance*, Kyoto Tsushinsha Press, Kyōto, 2008

Nitschke, Gunter, *Japanese Gardens*, Benedikt Tachen, Kőln, 1991

Sadler, A.L. *Japanese Tea Ceremony*, 1933; reprint, Charles E. Tuttle, Tōkyō and Rutland, VT, 2008

Suzuki, Daisetz, T., *Zen and Japanese Culture*, 1938; reprint, Princeton University Press, Princeton, NJ, 2010

Takei, Jiro and Marc P. Keane, *Sakuteiki: Visions of the Japanese garden*, Charles E. Tuttle, Tōkyō and Rutland, VT, 2008

Treib, Marc and Ron Herman, *Guide to the Gardens of Kyoto*, Kodansha International, Tōkyō, New York and London, 2003

Tschumi, Christian, *Mirei Shigemori: Modernizing the Japanese garden*, Stone Bridge Press, Berkeley, CA, 2005

Wright, Tom and Katsuhiko Mizuno, *Zen Gardens: Kyoto's nature enclosed*, Mitsumura Suiko Shoin, Kyōto, 1990

ACKNOWLEDGMENTS

I wish to thank for their great kindness and generosity the abbots and staff of Daisen-in, Daishin-in, Daitoku-ji, Entsū-ji, Entoku-in, Funda-in, Jikō-in, Keishun-in, Kennin-ji, Kōdai-ji, Kōmyō-in, Konchi-in, Kōtō-in, Nanzen-ji, Ōbai-in, Rokuō-in, Ryōan-ji, Ryōgen-in, Ryōgin-an, Saihō-ji, Shinju-an, Shōden-ji, Shūon-an, Tenryū-ji, Taizō-in, Tenju-an and Tōfuku-ji. Abbot Shōdō Maeda of Zuihō-in has, as always, been a wonderful source of inspiration as well as practical advice.

It has been a privilege to be able to work with Alex Ramsay. Having the opportunity of discussing these gardens with a photographer like Alex has been a precious experience. I am also very grateful to Sadao Hibi and Ian Korn for their kind permission to reproduce their photographs.

I would like to express my thanks to the production team who have worked on this book. At Frances Lincoln, my editors Andrew Dunn and Helen Griffin have been indefatigable in their efforts to improve the book. The designer Becky Clarke has been marvellous at marrying illustrations to text. I am grateful to Kathryn Pinker for her expertly rendered garden plans. My prose has benefited from Joanna Chisholm's meticulous editorial attention, and she has spared me many blushes. I also owe a debt of gratitude to Annelise Evans for her thorough scrutiny of my text.

I could not have written this book without the encouragement and support from my family and friends. I am deeply indebted to my parents, not least for their help on those days I needed to catch the first train in the morning to be in time for a photographic session at a temple. My husband, Simon Rees, has been unstinting in his support. He has challenged me with his critical insight, buoyed me with his enthusiasm, and borne patiently with the long anti-social hours I had to spend at my desk.

This book is dedicated to the memory of my late father-in-law, John Rees.

IMAGE CREDITS

All illustrations are by Kathryn Pinker.

All photographs copyright © Alex Ramsay, except for those listed below:

p8a Shutterstock © Morphart Creation
p8b Shutterstock © Stephen Rudolph
p8c Shutterstock © S. Borisov
p9a Shutterstock © Prill
p9c, 9d, 10a and 11b Shutterstock © Georgios Kollidas
p10b Shutterstock © CIS
p10c Shutterstock © Patrick Wang
p10d Shutterstock © Radka Palenikova
p11a Shutterstock © Vadim Kozlovsky
p11c Shutterstock © Matt Gibson
p46 Masterfile
p72–73 © Sadao Hibi
p78 lankphoto.com © Ian Korn
p101 Diomedia.com © MIXA
p106 Diomedia.com © JTB Photo / Takahashi Tsutomu;
p152 Diomedia.com © JTB Photo / Ogawa Yasutaka;
p187 Diomedia.com © JTB Photo / Kuroda Isao.